SCIENCE ENCYCLOPEDIAS

# THE BUG ENCYCLOPEDIA

BY MEG MARQUARDT

Abdo Reference

An Imprint of Abdo Publishing
abdobooks.com

# TABLE OF CONTENTS

**ALL ABOUT BUGS........................... 4**

**INSECTS**

American Cockroach.................... 8
American Grasshopper ............. 10
American Hoverfly ..................... 12
Antarctic Midge ......................... 14
Atlas Moth ................................. 16
Australian Walking Stick ........... 18
Bald-Faced Hornet ..................... 20
Bed Bug ...................................... 22
Black Carpenter Ant .................. 24
Blue Mud Dauber Wasp ............ 26
Boll Weevil ................................. 28
Brazilian Treehopper ................. 30
Brown Marmorated Stink Bug .............. 32
Bullet Ant ................................... 34
Common Green Bottle Fly ....... 36
Common Meadow Katydid ..... 38
Common Scorpion Fly .............. 40
Common Wasp........................... 42
Dead Leaf Butterfly ................... 44
Desert Locust ............................. 46
Dog Flea ..................................... 48
East African Lowland Honeybee.......... 50
Emerald Ash Borer .................... 52
Emerald Swallowtail Butterfly .............. 54
European Field Cricket ............. 56
European Mantis ....................... 58
Formosan Termite ..................... 60
Fruit Fly ...................................... 62
Giant Burrowing Cockroach .... 64
Giant Malaysian Leaf Insect .... 66

Giant Metallic Ceiba Borer ...... 68
Giant Stag Beetle ....................... 70
Glasswing Butterfly .................. 72
Golden Tortoise Beetle ............. 74
Green June Beetle ..................... 76
Green Peach Aphid ................... 78
Hercules Beetle .......................... 80
Honeybee ................................... 82
Housefly ..................................... 84
Hummingbird Hawk Moth ...... 86
Isabella Tiger Moth ................... 88
Japanese Beetle .......................... 90
Large Blue Cuckoo Wasp ......... 92
Little Barrier Giant Weta .......... 94
Luna Moth ................................. 96
Milkweed Assassin Bug ............ 98
Monarch Butterfly .................. 100
Northern Mole Cricket ........... 102
Northern Walking Stick ......... 104
Orchid Mantis ......................... 106
Painted Grasshopper .............. 108
Pharaoh Cicada ....................... 110
Rainbow Scarab Beetle .......... 112
Regal Moth .............................. 114
Rosemary Beetle ..................... 116
Rosy Maple Moth ................... 118
Saddleback Caterpillar Moth .......... 120
Seven-Spotted Ladybird ......... 122
Silverfish .................................. 124
Southern Flannel Moth .......... 126
Tarantula Hawk ...................... 128
Thorn Bug ............................... 130
Yellow Fever Mosquito .......... 132

## ARACHNIDS
Bird Dung Crab Spider .......................... 134
Black-Legged Tick ................................. 136
Brazilian Black Tarantula ..................... 138
Brown Recluse Spider .......................... 140
Camel Spider ......................................... 142
Daddy Longlegs .................................... 144
Deathstalker Scorpion ......................... 146
Emperor Scorpion ................................ 148
Giant Huntsman Spider ....................... 150
Giant Whip Scorpion ............................ 152
Goldenrod Crab Spider ....................... 154
Goliath Bird Spider ............................... 156
Indian Red Scorpion ............................. 158
Mexican Red Knee Tarantula .............. 160
Peacock Spider ..................................... 162
Peacock Tarantula ................................ 164
Two-Spotted Spider Mite .................... 166
Western Black Widow .......................... 168
Yellow Garden Spider ........................... 170

## CENTIPEDES
Amazonian Giant Centipede .............. 172
Bark Centipede ..................................... 174
Giant Desert Centipede ...................... 176
House Centipede .................................. 178

## MILLIPEDES
American Giant Millipede ................... 180
Giant African Millipede ....................... 182
Greenhouse Millipede ......................... 184
White-Legged Snake Millipede ......... 186

## GLOSSARY ............................................ 188
## TO LEARN MORE ................................. 189
## INDEX .................................................... 190
## PHOTO CREDITS ................................. 191

# ALL ABOUT BUGS

Bugs come in many shapes and sizes.

The world is full of bugs. Some crawl and some fly. Some burrow and others build elaborate webs. They live in all sorts of climates. Some can survive the extreme cold in Antarctica. Others live in tropical rain forests. Every creature has a unique and important role in its ecosystem.

The western black widow spider is a venomous arachnid.

Arthropoda is an animal group that includes insects, arachnids, centipedes, and millipedes. These animals are all called arthropods. People may refer to them as bugs. But insect scientists use the word *bug* to describe certain insects. Not all insects are bugs, and not all arthropods are insects. Arthropods are split into different categories based on the number of their legs and body parts. There are approximately 100,000 known arachnid species. The arachnid group includes spiders, scorpions, and ticks. An arachnid has eight legs and two body parts. Its lower body is called an abdomen. Some scorpions have abdomens that are long and end in tails. The abdomens of other arachnids, including some spider species, are shaped like big, round balls. The upper part of an arachnid's body is the cephalothorax. An arachnid's legs are attached to this part of the body.

The arthropods with the most legs are centipedes and millipedes. They typically have between 20 and 800 legs. Their bodies have many segments. Though centipedes and millipedes look similar to one another, there are key differences. They belong to different animal

The giant African millipede is the largest millipede species in the world.

groups. Centipedes are predators that eat other arthropods. Some of them even have venomous bites. Millipedes tend to eat plants. The groups have different leg shapes. Centipede feet are long and lie flat against the ground. They have one pair of legs per body segment. Millipede feet point downward. They have two pairs of legs per body segment. Scientists estimate that there are around 8,000 species of centipedes. However, they believe there are more than 80,000 species of millipedes.

Insects are the largest category of arthropods. There are one million known species of insects. The total number might be much higher, up to 30 million. Insects make up almost 90 percent of all animal life on Earth. Insects include beetles, butterflies, ants, and many more. Though insects come in many shapes and sizes, most of them have some basic anatomy in common. They have three parts to their bodies. They each have a head, a thorax in the middle, and an abdomen at the end. They have six legs. Many have antennae

Luna moths and other moth species are all types of insects.

on top of their heads, and most of them have wings.

One thing all of these animals have in common is that they don't have bones. They are invertebrates. Instead of a skeleton on the inside, arthropods have exoskeletons. An exoskeleton is made up of a hard material called chitin. It works like armor. But the exoskeleton cannot grow with the creature. In order to grow larger, an arthropod must molt, or shed, its exoskeleton.

Insects, arachnids, centipedes, and millipedes can be pests. Some may spread diseases and destroy crops. However, arthropods also play crucial roles in producing food and pollinating flowers. Some eat weeds. Others eat all sorts of dead things, which helps keep the environment clean. These creatures are essential parts of the world.

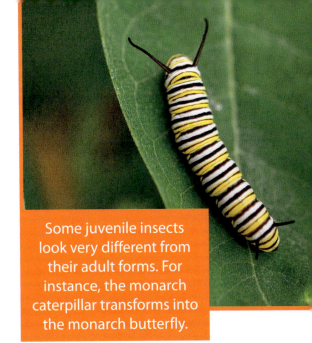

Some juvenile insects look very different from their adult forms. For instance, the monarch caterpillar transforms into the monarch butterfly.

Honeybees play important roles as pollinators.

# INSECTS
# AMERICAN COCKROACH (PERIPLANETA AMERICANA)

American cockroaches tend to live in humid or moist areas.

**A**merican cockroaches are the most common cockroach species in the world. They are reddish brown in color. They can live for almost three years, growing to about 1.5 inches (3.8 cm) long. They have wings that cover their entire backs. The wings of male cockroaches extend past their abdomens, making them slightly larger than females. An American cockroach molts between six and 14 times before it grows to its full size. It lives in dark, moist areas, such as basements and sewers.

Some cockroach species have survived for more than 300 million years. Part of their success is their diet. They eat a variety of foods, including decaying plant material. They also eat paper and leather boots.

### FACT BOX

**Range:** Worldwide
**Habitat:** Moist, dark places such as basements or sewers
**Diet:** Paper, leather, organic matter

American cockroaches, like other cockroach species, use their antennae to smell.

## INSECTS
# AMERICAN GRASSHOPPER (SCHISTOCERCA AMERICANA)

American grasshoppers are mostly green and brown. Those colors help them blend into the grasses and crops they eat. They can grow up to 2 inches (5 cm) long. They have long back legs. When sitting down, their back legs are higher than their abdomens. Their powerful legs help them launch high into the air. They also have wings and can fly more than 100 feet (30 m) at a time. Grasshoppers also use their legs to produce songs. Each grasshopper species produces a unique song.

An American grasshopper's color helps it blend in with its surroundings.

Some grasshoppers can travel nearly 4.3 feet (1.3 m) in a single jump.

All grasshopper species lay their eggs in soil. Young grasshoppers, called nymphs, hatch after three to four weeks. Nymphs do not have fully formed wings. They need to eat a lot of food in order to develop. They can eat so much that it causes major damage to crops like citrus trees.

**FACT BOX**

**Range:** United States, Mexico
**Habitat:** Dry, open spaces, such as farmlands and plains
**Diet:** Plants like corn, grasses, citrus trees

# INSECTS
# AMERICAN HOVERFLY (EUPEODES AMERICANUS)

Hoverflies, including the American hoverfly, look like bees but do not have stingers.

The yellow and black stripes on the American hoverfly give the insect the appearance of a bee. But it is actually a species of fly. Predators may confuse the American hoverfly for a bee, but it is harmless and cannot sting. American hoverflies are different from bees in other ways too. Bees have two sets of wings. American hoverflies have only one set of wings. Instead of a second pair of wings, the American hoverfly has a pair of small, club-shaped appendages called halteres that keep the fly stable while flying. Halteres also allow the insect to hover in place and to fly backward, which most other insects cannot do. The American hoverfly has large eyes and stubby antennae.

Adult and juvenile hoverflies have different diets. As adults, hoverflies drink nectar from flowering plants. They help with pollination. Juvenile hoverflies eat aphids. Aphids are small, green insects that often harm crops. Larval hoverflies eat so many aphids that they save crops from damage.

**FACT BOX**
**Range:** North America
**Habitat:** Flowering plants
**Diet:** Nectar as adults, aphids as larvae

American hoverflies are important pollinators.

# INSECTS
# ANTARCTIC MIDGE (BELGICA ANTARCTICA)

The Antarctic midge is one of three insect species known to live on Antarctica. It is less than 0.4 inches (1 cm) long, has no wings, and is all black. Because Antarctica has such a harsh environment, this midge has developed amazing survival abilities. It spends more than nine months of the year frozen. It can even survive a whole month without oxygen. Antarctica gets more ultraviolet light from the sun than most places on Earth. This form of light can cause health issues. But the Antarctic midge can survive high exposure to these rays.

Antarctic midges mate when they are adults.

Scientists study Antarctic midge larvae to understand how the insects survive in the harsh climate.

Antarctic midge larvae are also able to withstand the extreme conditions. They can lose up to 70 percent of the water in their bodies and still survive. An Antarctic midge spends two years in the larval stage. It lives for about ten days in its adult stage.

**FACT BOX**
**Range:** Antarctica
**Habitat:** Underground
**Diet:** Algae, bacteria

## INSECTS
# ATLAS MOTH (ATTACUS ATLAS)

The Atlas moth has one of the largest wingspans of all insects. Its wings can stretch more than 10 inches (25 cm). They are shades of brown, red, white, and black. Their wings startle predators. The tip of each wing looks like a cobra head. If a predator comes too close, the moth will flash its wings open. Atlas moths have been known to drop to the ground and thrash in order to look more like a snake.

The Atlas moth caterpillar is green. It blends in with its leafy habitat. This species can eat only when it is a caterpillar. Adult moths have tiny mouthparts that do not work. Because they can't eat, Atlas moths do not move much as adults in order to conserve energy. The food the caterpillars

The spots on the Atlas moth's wings startle predators.

eat provides enough energy for the moth to survive for about two weeks. During this time, the moth finds a mate and reproduces.

### FACT BOX

**Range**: Southeast Asia
**Habitat**: Rain forests
**Diet**: Nothing as adults, leaves as young

Atlas moth caterpillars spray a stinky odor at predators.

# INSECTS
# AUSTRALIAN WALKING STICK (EXTATOSOMA TIARATUM)

An Australian walking stick may eat its skin after it molts.

The Australian walking stick lives in eucalyptus trees. It eats leaves from this tree. Over time, the species has evolved to closely resemble the tree's twigs. The Australian walking stick is light brown. Males grow to around 4 inches (10 cm) long. Females can grow up to 5 inches (12.7 cm). The Australian walking stick has wide, flat growth on its legs that looks like dead leaves. Its curled tail also looks like a large dead leaf. But despite its leafy appearance, the Australian walking stick has a hard exoskeleton. Its back legs have spikes that help the insect fight off predators. The Australian walking stick kicks its spiky legs at predators that come too close. This is an important defense, especially for females. Males can fly, but females cannot. Females rely on spikes and blending in to stay safe from predators.

## FACT BOX
**Range**: Australia
**Habitat**: Eucalyptus trees
**Diet**: Eucalyptus leaves

Australian walking sticks have suction pads on the bottoms of their feet that help them climb.

# INSECTS
## BALD-FACED HORNET (DOLICHOVESPULA MACULATA)

Bald-faced hornets are pollinators.

The bald-faced hornet has striking facial features. While the top of its head is black, the front of its face is bright white. It also has white on its abdomen and the point of its thorax. Its wings are dark brown. It grows between 0.5 to 0.75 inches (1.2 to 1.9 cm) long.

These hornets chew on woody material. The wood mixes with their saliva, forming a pulp that they use to make their nests. Bald-faced hornets live in colonies. A single nest may have 400 individuals. Adult hornets have specialized roles. The queen lays eggs. Workers may repair the nest and help feed larvae. They also defend the nest from predators. These hornets have smooth stingers that allow them to sting multiple times. The stinger injects venom, which can be painful. These hornets can also spray venom into the eyes of predators.

### FACT BOX
**Range:** North America
**Habitat:** Trees, shrubs
**Diet:** Nectar as adults, other insects as young

A bald-faced hornet nest can be as large as 3 feet (0.9 m) wide.

## INSECTS
# BED BUG *(CIMEX LECTULARIUS)*

Bed bugs have flat, brown, oval bodies. They are tiny. Adults are smaller than 0.25 inches (0.6 cm) long. Because they are so small, they can hide in mattresses or under beds. Bed bugs are pests. They drink blood. They prefer human blood but will drink blood from cats, dogs, and other warm-blooded animals. Bed bugs are nocturnal, meaning they are more active at night. They may feed on a sleeping person for up to ten minutes. After being bitten, a person may develop itchy, red welts. But bed bugs are not known to spread disease.

A bed bug's flat body helps it hide in folds of fabric.

Chemicals in a bed bug's saliva reduce pain and increase blood flow. This helps them avoid detection from the host animal.

It can be hard to get rid of bed bugs once they have infested a home. A female may lay hundreds of eggs over her life span. Bed bugs can hide in small cracks. They can survive for months without food. It usually takes a professional pest controller to get rid of them all.

### FACT BOX
**Range**: Worldwide
**Habitat**: Houses, bird nests, bat caves
**Diet**: Blood

## INSECTS
# BLACK CARPENTER ANT (CAMPONOTUS PENNSYLVANICUS)

Black carpenter ants chew through wood, but they do not eat it.

Black carpenter ants live in large societies. A black carpenter ant colony can have more than 3,000 members. The colony has workers that gather food and build nests. There is one queen per colony. Most of the ants are wingless. But when a colony becomes large, some ants are born with wings. These ants can fly off to start their own colonies.

Black carpenter ants are large for ants. They grow to around 0.75 inches (1.9 cm) long. They are named for their nest-building skills. They chew tunnels into wood such as decaying logs. They can also chew through wood in houses and cause damage.

These ants have a special relationship with aphids. Aphids produce a sweet dew that black carpenter ants eat. Black carpenter ants will feed and protect these aphids. This way the ants will have a supply of the dew.

**FACT BOX**
**Range:** Eastern North America
**Habitat:** Wooded areas, near homes
**Diet:** Plants, insects, dew from aphids

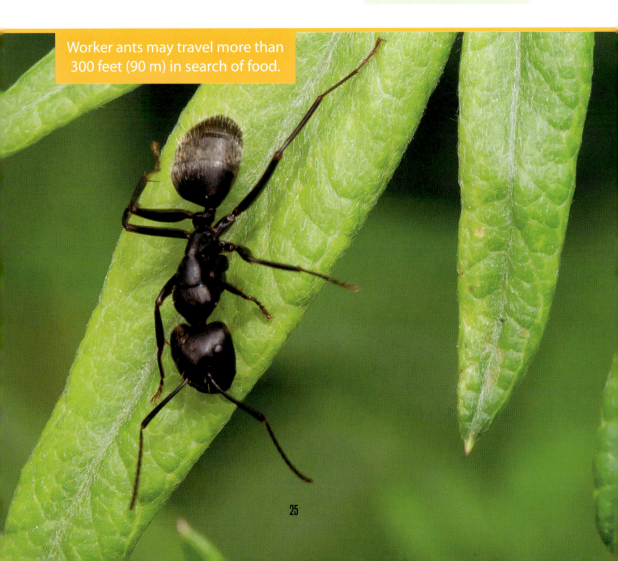

Worker ants may travel more than 300 feet (90 m) in search of food.

## INSECTS
# BLUE MUD DAUBER WASP (CHALYBION CALIFORNICUM)

**B**lue mud dauber wasps are a metallic blue-black color. They grow to around 1 inch (2.5 cm) long. These wasps do not build their own nests. Instead, they take over mud nests built by other wasps. The nests contain many tunnels and rooms. A blue mud dauber will use water to reshape the nests. It will kill other creatures in the nest and destroy the eggs. Then it sets up its own nursery. This starts with gathering spiders. Blue mud daubers are known for attacking black widow spiders. They sting the spider and inject it with venom, paralyzing the spider.

Unlike other wasp species, the blue mud dauber wasp is a solitary creature.

Nectar is the main source of food for adult blue mud dauber wasps.

The mud dauber wasp then drags the spider to the nest. A female lays her eggs. Then she seals off the room. When the eggs hatch, the larvae eat the spider as a first meal.

## FACT BOX

**Range**: Mexico, California
**Habitat**: Wherever there are flowers and water
**Diet**: Nectar as adults, spiders as young

## INSECTS
# BOLL WEEVIL (ANTHONOMUS GRANDIS)

A boll weevil lives for about three weeks.

The boll weevil has a round body and a long snout. The beetle grows only to about 0.25 inches (0.6 cm) long. A quarter of its length comes from its snout. An adult's body is gray or black, which matches the color of the cotton plant it lives on. Female boll weevils lay eggs in cotton plant buds. Boll weevils lay around 300 eggs at one time. There may be ten generations of boll weevils in a single year. The larvae will eat every part of the cotton plant. These pests can become a big problem for farmers. If a farm has an infestation, it may lose its entire crop.

Boll weevils originated in Mexico. They arrived in the United States in the 1800s. They spread quickly. Boll weevils have destroyed more than $13 billion worth of cotton since their arrival in the United States.

**FACT BOX**
**Range:** Mexico, Central America, southeastern United States
**Habitat:** Cotton fields
**Diet:** Cotton

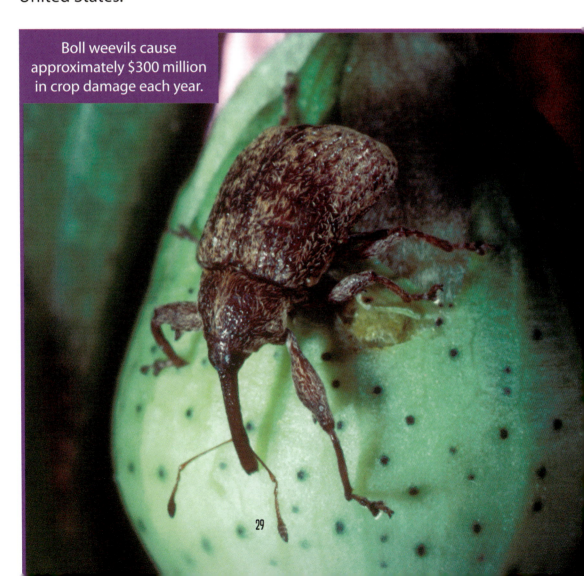

Boll weevils cause approximately $300 million in crop damage each year.

# INSECTS
## BRAZILIAN TREEHOPPER (BOCYDIUM GLOBULARE)

The Brazilian treehopper is a small insect about the size of a pea. It has a unique, rod-like structure that grows out of its head. At the top, the rod splits into five parts. Four of the parts end in a small ball that is covered with hair. The fifth part grows parallel to the treehopper's back. Scientists are not sure of the purpose of this head structure, but they have a few theories. The shape might trick predators into biting the structure rather than the head itself. It might also mimic a parasitic fungus. Some insects can become infected with fungi that burst out of the insect's head. Predators know to avoid bugs with that shape. They may leave the Brazilian treehopper alone because they believe the insect is infected.

Brazilian treehoppers suck sap from stems and leaves.

Predators may avoid Brazilian treehoppers because they look similar to insects that are infected with fungus, *pictured*.

Other treehopper species also have structures that grow out of their heads. They may resemble thorns or leaves.

## FACT BOX

**Range:** South America
**Habitat:** Rain forests
**Diet:** Tree sap

# INSECTS
# BROWN MARMORATED STINK BUG (HALYOMORPHA HALYS)

Brown marmorated stink bug nymphs have black heads and red bodies.

The brown marmorated stink bug has a distinctive body shape that looks like a shield. This insect is mostly brown and white and grows to be 0.6 inches (1.5 cm) long. Stink bugs get their name from a smelly odor they produce when threatened. Some humans are allergic to the chemicals in the odor.

Brown marmorated stink bugs are more than just a smelly problem. They are also an invasive species. They are native to Asia and were first spotted in the United States in the late 1990s.

## FACT BOX
**Range:** Asia, United States
**Habitat:** Wooded areas, fields
**Diet:** Fruits, nuts, vegetables

The insects likely traveled overseas on a shipping container. Since then, they have spread quickly throughout the eastern and midwestern United States. They have also been seen on the West Coast. These stink bugs can infest farmlands. They especially like fruit trees. They cause millions of dollars in damage each year. Brown marmorated stink bugs may be found in homes during the fall and winter. Thousands of stink bugs may gather in a single home to wait out the cold.

The brown marmorated stink bug eats fruits and leaves from a variety of crops.

## INSECTS
# BULLET ANT (PARAPONERA CLAVATA)

The bullet ant is large compared to other ant species. It can grow up to 1.2 inches (3 cm) long. Like other ants, bullet ants live in colonies of thousands. Bullet ants have large jaws and noticeable stingers. They are usually not aggressive, but they sting

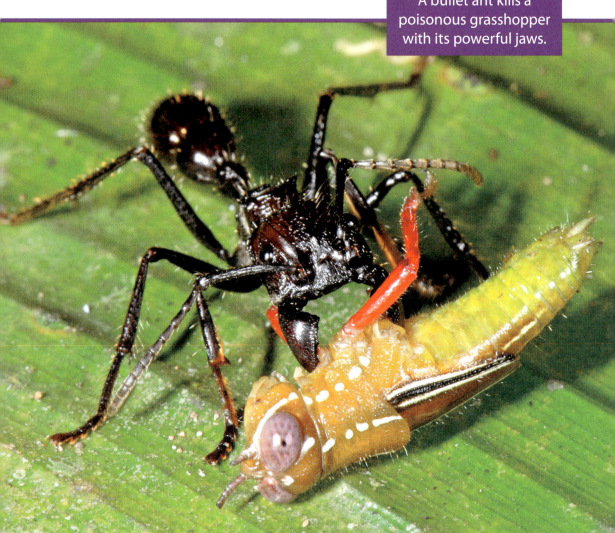

A bullet ant kills a poisonous grasshopper with its powerful jaws.

Bullet ants are one of the largest ant species in size.

when threatened. Some people consider the bullet ant sting to be the most painful insect sting in the world. The pain can last for up to 24 hours. The ants are named for the painful sting. Some have compared the pain to being shot with a bullet.

The bullet ant releases chemicals when it stings. The chemicals signal nearby bullet ants to sting the target as well. The stings do not cause lasting damage to humans. They cause shaking and nausea that eventually go away. But the stings are lethal to other insects. The venom is strong enough to kill or paralyze prey.

**FACT BOX**
**Range**: Amazon rain forest
**Habitat**: Forests
**Diet**: Small insects

## INSECTS
# COMMON GREEN BOTTLE FLY (LUCILIA SERICATA)

Common green bottle flies have bright-green bodies and red eyes. They grow to around 0.4 inches (1 cm) long. These flies have hair on their backs near their heads. They are scavengers. They eat dead animals. They also cluster around rotting garbage looking for food. These flies play important roles in their ecosystems. They break down decaying materials. They help nutrients from dead plants and animals return to the soil.

Common green bottle flies help people too. They are important to forensics. This is the field of science that focuses on solving crimes. Because common green bottle flies feed on decaying flesh, they are often found on dead human bodies. Forensic scientists look for the presence of these flies. They can estimate how long a person has been dead based on how old the flies are. These flies also play a role in medicine. When other treatments do not work, doctors place the larvae of these flies on a person's wound. The larvae eat away the dead tissue. This helps healthy tissue grow.

Bottle flies have compound eyes. Each eye is made of hundreds of individual eyes.

### FACT BOX
**Range:** Northern hemisphere
**Habitat:** Rotting things, such as garbage or dead animals
**Diet:** Carcasses, dung

Common green bottle flies have a metallic appearance.

## INSECTS
# COMMON MEADOW KATYDID *(ORCHELIMUM VULGARE)*

The common meadow katydid is a pale-green color. It has small, reddish-orange eyes. These katydids are usually around 1.3 inches (3.3 cm) long. Common meadow katydids have strong jaws that help them eat tough plant material.

All female katydids have a long, horn-shaped structure that extends from the back of their abdomens. This structure helps them place their eggs. Females lay eggs inside hollow plants. When larvae hatch from the eggs, they eat their way out of the plant.

Many people confuse katydids for grasshoppers. These two insect groups

The common meadow katydid produces ticking sounds followed by a loud buzz.

Unlike some insect species, a young katydid, *pictured*, looks similar to an adult.

share some features. Some katydids and grasshoppers have similar coloring. Both types of insects have wings and long back legs. But there are differences too. Katydids have wings, but they cannot fly. They use their wings to communicate through song. Katydids have longer antennae than grasshoppers. These insects also lay their eggs in different areas. Katydids lay eggs in plants. Grasshoppers bury their eggs in soil.

**FACT BOX**

**Range**: United States, Canada
**Habitat**: Fields, meadows
**Diet**: Mostly leaves, but also fruits and dead insects

# INSECTS
# COMMON SCORPION FLY (PANORPA COMMUNIS)

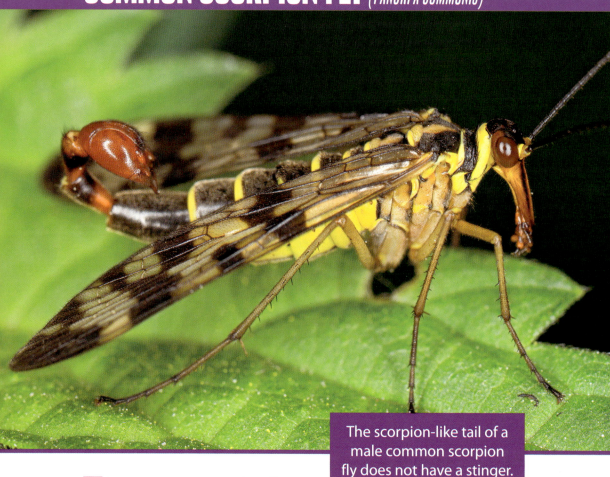

The scorpion-like tail of a male common scorpion fly does not have a stinger.

The common scorpion fly is named for its tail, which curls upward and is a reddish-brown color. The tail looks like a scorpion tail, but it does not sting. Only male scorpion flies have this structure. The tail has reproductive organs. Male common scorpion flies also use their tails to attract a mate. As part of the mating ritual, males will present females with a gift. The gift may be a drop of the male's saliva or a dead insect to eat. Mating is dangerous for the male. The female might decide to kill the potential mate. After mating, the female lays eggs in soil.

The common scorpion fly is around 1.2 inches (3 cm) long. It is yellow and black with dark spots on its wings. It has a reddish head and a long snout. The snout helps it eat dead insects. The common scorpion fly is a scavenger. It is known to steal dead insects from spiderwebs.

**FACT BOX**
**Range**: Europe
**Habitat**: Woods, bushes
**Diet**: Dead insects

Common scorpion flies will sometimes drink nectar, though they prefer dead insects.

## INSECTS
# COMMON WASP (VESPULA VULGARIS)

Common wasp nests may have a honeycomb-shaped structure.

The common wasp has a black and yellow body. It has a triangular head with thick antennae. Its wings are thin and black. It typically grows to 0.78 inches (2 cm) long.

Common wasps are important pollinators. As adults, these wasps drink nectar. They collect and deposit pollen as they travel between flowers. This helps plants reproduce. Sugar provides the wasps with a lot of energy. In addition to nectar, sugar-rich foods like fruits and soda can attract adult common wasps. Juveniles eat insects. They help limit pests such as aphids and caterpillars.

But colonies of common wasps can be considered pests themselves. Common wasps chew up wood to make a papery pulp for their nests. They may build their nests in urban areas. Common wasp nests are often found under decks or roofs. There can be more than 5,000 wasps in one nest. They may sting people who disturb their nests.

**FACT BOX**
**Range:** Europe, Southeast Asia, Australia
**Habitat:** Woodlands, urban areas
**Diet:** Nectar and sugary foods as adults, insects as young

Rotting fruit attracts common wasps.

## INSECTS
# DEAD LEAF BUTTERFLY (KALLIMA INACHUS)

The dead leaf butterfly has a wingspan of about 3 inches (7.6 cm). The tops of its wings are blue or violet. The color changes depending on the season. The undersides of its wings are brown.

This butterfly is best known for its camouflage ability. Its wings are an important adaptation. When it closes its wings, the butterfly looks like a dead leaf. The appearance of these butterflies varies throughout the year. The color and pattern of the wings look different depending on whether it is

The tops and bottoms of a dead leaf butterfly's wings are different colors.

Dead leaf butterflies may hide near leaves on the ground.

the rainy season or the dry season. During the rainy season, most dead leaf butterflies have wings that look like wet leaves. During the dry season, most of them have wings that look like crisp, dry leaves. The butterflies that best blend into their surroundings are most likely to survive.

Dead leaf butterflies move erratically when they are flying. They look like leaves being blown by the wind. This helps them escape from predators. They may fly toward the ground to hide in leaves.

**FACT BOX**

**Range:** Southeast Asia
**Habitat:** Leaf litter, trees
**Diet:** Rotting fruits, dung

# INSECTS
# DESERT LOCUST *(SCHISTOCERCA GREGARIA)*

A swarm of desert locusts can cover more than 460 square miles (1,190 sq km).

Desert locusts are related to grasshoppers. Both have long back legs. Desert locusts are mostly green, brown, and black. They can grow up to 3 inches (7.6 cm) long.

Desert locusts may gather in swarms of more than 80 million. When swarming, desert locusts change their behaviors. Their appetites increase. They work together as a social group to find food. Locust swarms can cause a lot of damage. A desert locust can eat its entire body weight in plants each day. A large swarm may eat the same amount of food as 35,000 people. These insects can also travel a great distance in a short period of time. They can fly 90 miles (145 km) in a single day. In 2020, the World Bank estimated that desert locust swarms caused $8.5 billion in damage in Yemen and East Africa alone.

**FACT BOX**
**Range:** Africa, Asia
**Habitat:** Deserts, farmlands
**Diet:** Plants

Climate change is causing locust swarms to become larger and more frequent. Some desert areas are getting more rain than they have in the past. This has led to a desert locust population boom.

Desert locusts cause severe damage to crops.

# INSECTS
# DOG FLEA (CTENOCEPHALIDES CANIS)

The dog flea is a parasite that is commonly found on dogs. But it can attach to many kinds of mammals, including cats, foxes, and rats. People can also have these fleas. Dogs or cats that live outdoors are more likely to pick up dog fleas. An animal can quickly become infested with these insects and may lose large amounts of blood as a result. That's because the dog flea—like many other flea species—drinks blood from mammals. In addition, these fleas can carry bacteria that cause disease. When dog fleas bite into another animal, bacteria may

Dog fleas are very small. They are difficult to see without a microscope.

Some flea species can drink 15 times their weight in blood.

enter the bloodstream. This can cause severe illness. Luckily, there are ways to control these pests. Flea collars, flea baths, and flea combs help owners keep their pets safe.

**FACT BOX**
**Range:** Worldwide
**Habitat:** On mammals, both domestic and wild
**Diet:** Blood

Dog fleas are small, reddish-brown insects. They grow to only around 0.13 inches (0.35 cm) long. They have long legs relative to their bodies. This helps them jump. Some flea species can jump up to 12 inches (30 cm). Flea species reproduce quickly. A female flea lays about 30 eggs every day.

# INSECTS
# EAST AFRICAN LOWLAND HONEYBEE (APIS MELLIFERA SCUTELLATA)

Pollen sticks to the hairs on an east African lowland honeybee's body.

The East African lowland honeybee is a subspecies of the honeybee. It looks very similar to other honeybees. It has yellow and black stripes and clear wings. This subspecies is smaller in size than other populations of honeybees. Adults grow to be about 0.75 inches (1.9 cm) long.

East African lowland honeybees are native to Africa. But they were brought to Brazil in the 1950s to help with pollination. A swarm of East African lowland honeybees was accidentally released. These bees began to reproduce with other honeybees in the region. This produced a type of bee known as the Africanized bee. All honeybees will protect their hives, but Africanized bees are especially aggressive. Hundreds of them may attack an intruder at once. This type of bee also takes over other bee colonies. They share food with other bees. This helps them become accepted into the new colony. Eventually, the Africanized honeybee queen takes over the colony. This behavior has helped the subspecies spread throughout South and Central America.

## FACT BOX

**Range:** Africa, Central America, South America, North America
**Habitat:** Anywhere they can build a nest
**Diet:** Nectar, pollen

East African lowland honeybees are important pollinators.

## INSECTS
# EMERALD ASH BORER (AGRILUS PLANIPENNIS)

Emerald ash borers have spread quickly throughout the United States since 2002.

The emerald ash borer is a brilliant green color. It has a metallic appearance. It is a type of beetle that typically grows to 0.5 inches (1.3 cm) long. The emerald ash borer is native to Asia. It was first discovered in the United States in 2002 and is an invasive species there. The beetle was likely accidentally carried into the country in wooden packing materials. It has spread to at least 35 US states and Canada.

Since its arrival in the United States, the emerald ash borer has destroyed tens to hundreds of millions of ash trees.

A female emerald ash borer lays its eggs inside the bark of an ash tree. The larvae bore, or tunnel, through the tree to feed. This damages the tree. It makes it difficult for the tree to get water and nutrients. Most trees die within a couple years of infestation. Trees that have been infested by these beetles begin to lose their upper branches. There are *D*-shaped holes in the bark where the insect exited the tree. Infested trees attract woodpeckers. Woodpeckers strip off tree bark to find prey, further damaging trees.

**FACT BOX**

**Range**: Asia, United States, Canada
**Habitat**: Woodland forests
**Diet**: Leaves as adults, ash trees as larvae

Feeding trails in ash trees are one sign of an emerald ash borer infestation.

## INSECTS
# EMERALD SWALLOWTAIL BUTTERFLY (PAPILIO PALINURUS)

The emerald swallowtail butterfly gets its name for the bright-green band on its otherwise black wings. The wings appear to glitter. At certain angles, the wings may look blue or yellow. The color of the wings shifts depending on how the light hits the wings. This is called iridescence. The butterfly's wings are made of tiny scales. These scales reflect light in a way that causes the wings to shimmer. The emerald swallowtail is a relatively large butterfly. It has a wingspan of 4 inches (10 cm). This butterfly is native to Southeast Asia, but it is also raised in butterfly houses around the world.

The emerald swallowtail caterpillar is not as beautiful as its adult form. It looks like bird droppings. It also has scent

The emerald swallowtail butterfly pollinates flowers as it drinks nectar.

Emerald swallowtails are raised in butterfly houses because of their beauty.

glands that cause it to smell bad. It produces an odor when it is in danger. These adaptations help protect emerald swallowtail caterpillars from predators. Some farmers consider these caterpillars to be pests because they feed on citrus plants.

### FACT BOX

**Range:** Southeast Asia
**Habitat:** Trees
**Diet:** Nectar as a butterfly, citrus trees and plants as caterpillars

# INSECTS
# EUROPEAN FIELD CRICKET (GRYLLUS CAMPESTRIS)

European field crickets are found in Europe. They live in burrows underground. Nymphs hibernate in burrows during the winter. Field crickets do not typically grow larger than 1 inch (2.5 cm) long.

European field crickets have wings, which are used for song rather than flight. The wings of these male crickets have special veins called harps. When they rub their legs against the harps, they produce a chirping sound. This sound attracts females and is mostly commonly heard on summer evenings. But as the years pass, this chirping sound has become rarer. That's because the European field cricket is endangered. The species is threatened by habitat loss. As humans develop land, the fields and burrows that European

European field crickets have dark bodies and golden wings.

**FACT BOX**
**Range:** Europe
**Habitat:** Fields, lawns
**Diet:** Plants, insects

field crickets live in are destroyed. In 1980, there may have been fewer than 100 European field crickets left in the United Kingdom. But scientists today work to protect these crickets. They raise crickets on a reserve to help restore their numbers.

Female field crickets lay their eggs in a burrow after mating.

## INSECTS
# EUROPEAN MANTIS (MANTIS RELIGIOSA)

The European mantis is brown and green, and its head is shaped like a triangle. This insect is around 2.4 inches (6 cm) long. Females are larger and heavier than males. Even though both females and males have wings, only the males can fly. Males also have larger eyes and longer antennae than females. Mating can be dangerous for males. A female may kill and eat a male that tries to mate with her.

The European mantis is sometimes called a praying mantis. That is because it often crouches with its front legs folded.

A European mantis can turn its head 180 degrees.

It looks like the bug is praying. But the European mantis is a deadly predator. It hides and waits for a meal to come by. Then it unfolds its legs with rapid speed, surprising the prey. It can grab flying insects, such as grasshoppers, out of the air to eat. The undersides of the front legs are covered with spikes. This gives the mantis a strong grip. It is difficult for the prey to escape.

A European mantis spreads its wings so that it appears larger. This can scare away predators.

## FACT BOX

**Range**: Europe, United States
**Habitat**: Meadows
**Diet**: Caterpillars, moths, grasshoppers

# INSECTS
# FORMOSAN TERMITE (COPTOTERMES FORMOSANUS)

Formosan termites are tiny, only about 0.6 inches (1.5 cm) long. They gather in colonies that can contain several million individuals. The colonies are made up of three types of members. The first group is the workers. They are pale whitish in color. The second group is soldiers. They are the protectors of the nest. They have orangish heads and large mandibles. The third group is the reproductive group. It includes the king, the queen, and termite nymphs.

Formosan termites, like other termite species, have different jobs within the colony.

A Formosan termite colony may eat 1,000 pounds (450 kg) of wood each year.

Originally from Asia, Formosan termites were first discovered in the United States in 1957. They eat wood and can cause extreme damage to homes and buildings. Some experts estimate that these termites cause more than $1 billion in damage in the United States each year. Formosan termite colonies are larger than colonies of other termite species. Their colonies can grow to cover 164 feet (50 m) of land. Eventually, some areas of the large colony may split off. These sections are called buds, and the Formosan termites there will let unrelated termites come into their buds.

**FACT BOX**
**Range:** Southeast Asia, southeastern United States
**Habitat:** Underground, in houses
**Diet:** Wood

# INSECTS
## FRUIT FLY (DROSOPHILA MELANOGASTER)

Fruit fly larvae can become fully grown in less than a week. This allows an infestation to grow quickly.

Fruit flies grow to about 0.1 inch (0.3 cm) long. They have black and tan bodies. Their eyes are often bright red, but they can come in many different colors. Fruit flies are common household pests. They are attracted to ripening fruit, which is where they lay their eggs. A fruit fly can lay approximately 500 eggs during its life. An infestation can grow quickly.

Fruit flies also play an important role in science. Fruit flies and humans have many genes in common. Genes determine traits such as eye color and height. Genes may also cause certain diseases. Scientists study the fruit flies. They can breed flies to have certain genes. Since fruit flies are able to reproduce quickly, scientists can study many flies with those genes. They study the appearance and behavior of the flies. They use the flies as a model to understand the role of genes in disease and animal behavior.

**FACT BOX**

**Range:** Worldwide
**Habitat:** Gardens, kitchens, other areas with ripe fruits
**Diet:** Fermenting fruits

Scientists can breed fruit flies to have different eye colors.

## INSECTS
# GIANT BURROWING COCKROACH (MACROPANESTHIA RHINOCEROS)

The giant burrowing cockroach has long, sensitive antennae.

Giant burrowing cockroaches can grow to around 3 inches (7.6 cm) long. They are about the size of an adult palm. They are the heaviest cockroach species, weighing about 1 ounce (30 g). These cockroaches are dark brown and have spiky legs. They use their legs like shovels to burrow underground. They may dig as deep as 3 feet (1 m) under the surface. Their burrows can be as long as 18 feet (6 m). Giant burrowing cockroaches hiss by pushing air out of their abdomens.

Compared to other insects, giant burrowing cockroaches have a long life span. They can live for ten years. Many insects lay eggs. But these cockroaches give birth to live young. A female burrowing cockroach will build a nursery at the end of her burrow. She takes care of her young for about six months. She feeds them leaf litter during this time.

**FACT BOX**
**Range**: Australia
**Habitat**: Underground
**Diet**: Eucalyptus leaves

Giant burrowing cockroaches typically live alone. They meet up only to mate.

# INSECTS
## GIANT MALAYSIAN LEAF INSECT (PHYLLIUM GIGANTEUM)

Giant Malaysian leaf insects grow to be 4 inches (10 cm) long. They can cover the palm of an adult hand. Their bodies and legs look just like leaves. Juvenile and adult giant Malaysian leaf insects are different colors. The young are all brown. They spend most of their time on the forest floor. Their color helps them blend in with dead leaves. Adults are mostly a pale green. They have brown spots and edges. This makes their leafy camouflage even more realistic. They are able to hide from predators. Giant Malaysian leaf insects even move in ways that make them appear leaf-like. They will sway from side to side if there is a breeze. They move very slowly to avoid being seen

The giant Malaysian leaf insect is a herbivore and only eats tree leaves.

The giant Malaysian leaf insect is more active at night.

by predators. Their camouflage is so convincing that these insects may accidentally eat each other.

The majority of giant Malaysian leaf insects are female. They can reproduce asexually. This means that they don't need males to fertilize their eggs. The unfertilized eggs still develop and hatch.

**FACT BOX**

**Range**: Malaysia
**Habitat**: Fruit trees
**Diet**: Leaves of fruit trees

## INSECTS
# GIANT METALLIC CEIBA BORER (EUCHROMA GIGANTEA)

The giant metallic ceiba borer belongs to a family of bugs called jewel beetles. These beetles are known for their brilliantly colored bodies. The giant metallic ceiba borer is no exception. It has a green head. Its back gleams like polished metal. It is gold, bronze, green, and purple. It has large, black eyes and can grow to more than 3 inches (7.6 cm) long.

The ceiba borer secretes chemicals to protect it from the sun and keep it moist.

The ceiba borer's thick wing cases protect it from predators.

Male metallic ceiba borers make a clicking noise. This sound is part of the mating process. It attracts females. After mating, a female metallic ceiba borer will look for a damaged tree in which to lay her eggs. Larvae feed on decaying matter. They take approximately two years to develop into adults. As larvae, they remain in the tree they hatched in. They do not develop wings until they are adults. Then they can fly between trees.

**FACT BOX**
**Range:** Central America, South America, southern United States
**Habitat:** High in trees
**Diet:** Leaves and pollen as adults, dying tree parts as young

# INSECTS
# GIANT STAG BEETLE (LUCANUS ELAPHUS)

The giant stag beetle is a brownish-red color. It is more active at night, and its color helps it blend in with the forest. The giant stag beetle usually crawls on the ground. But it has wings. It may fly toward lights at night. Adults can rub their wings together to make sound.

The giant stag beetle grows to 2 inches (5 cm) long. It has a striking appearance. Male stag beetles have two huge mandibles. They look like deer antlers and make up about half of the beetle's length. Female mandibles are much smaller. Males use their mandibles to fight each other. The winning male mates with a female.

Adults and larvae live together in colonies. Females lay their eggs in rotting wood that the larvae will eventually eat. These insects help return nutrients to the soil.

Habitat destruction threatens the giant stag beetle.

Male giant stag beetles will fly in search of a mate.

### FACT BOX

**Range:** North America
**Habitat:** Forests
**Diet:** Sap as adults, rotting wood as young

## INSECTS
# GLASSWING BUTTERFLY (GRETA OTO)

Most butterflies have colorful wings. Glasswing butterfly wings are orange, white, and black along the edges. But most of the wing is transparent. This helps the butterfly blend into its surroundings. The glasswing butterfly has a wingspan of about 2 inches (5 cm). The wings have a special structure. Most butterfly wings are made of tiny scales that reflect light. But reflective wings would make glasswing butterflies easy to spot. Their wings are covered with tiny hairs instead. This makes their wings less shiny.

Glasswing butterfly chrysalises become transparent when the butterfly is ready to hatch.

Glasswing butterflies may fly as far as 12 miles (19 km) in a single day.

Glasswing butterflies can fly quickly. They can fly at 8 miles per hour (13 kmh) for short periods of time. They are also very strong. They can carry up to 40 times their body weight.

Glasswing caterpillars are green with purple and red stripes. They feed on nightshade plants. These plants are toxic to humans and many other animals. But over time, the caterpillars have adapted to handle the toxins. They store the toxins in their bodies. This prevents most predators from eating them.

**FACT BOX**

**Range:** South America, Central America
**Habitat:** Rain forests
**Diet:** Nectar as adults, nightshade plants as caterpillars

# INSECTS
# GOLDEN TORTOISE BEETLE (CHARIDOTELLA SEXPUNCTATA)

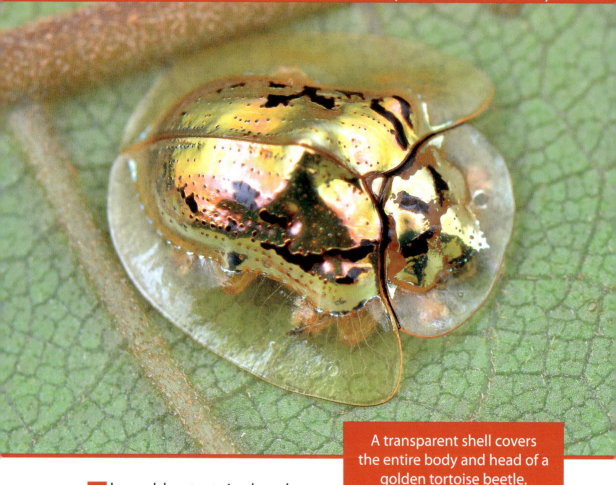

A transparent shell covers the entire body and head of a golden tortoise beetle.

The golden tortoise beetle has a gold, metallic appearance. It is a round beetle with a transparent shell. It grows to be around 0.3 inches (0.7 cm) long. These beetles have the ability to change color. They respond to their environments. Scientists first observed that the beetles changed colors when mating. Their bodies would turn to a brownish-orange color with black spots. Golden tortoise beetles also change in appearance when startled or stressed.

Scientists believe this color change may work like camouflage. The beetles can appear dull orange with black spots. This pattern makes the golden tortoise beetle look like a ladybird. Predators such as birds do not like to eat ladybirds. They may leave the golden tortoise beetle alone.

Golden tortoise beetles may be seen in gardens. They eat plants like morning glories and sweet potatoes. They lay eggs on the undersides of plant leaves. Larvae hatch after about ten days. They have a spine on their rear ends called an anal fork. They use the anal fork to hold molted skin or poop. These materials can be used as a shield to protect against predators.

Golden tortoise beetles can change color in two minutes.

### FACT BOX

**Range:** North America
**Habitat:** Gardens
**Diet:** Sweet potato and morning glory vines

## INSECTS
# GREEN JUNE BEETLE (COTINIS NITIDA)

The green June beetle has a bright-green shell. It has brown stripes along its back and sides. These beetles grow to be around 1 inch (2.5 cm) long. They hatch during the summer months. A large group of beetles may hatch at once. The larvae, also known as grubs, can be very destructive. The grubs develop underground. During the winter, they secrete a substance that causes soil to stick together. The soil forms

Green June beetles eat peaches and other fruits.

Green June beetle larvae hatch from eggs after ten to 15 days.

protective cases around the developing larvae. As they get older, these grubs can damage lawns. They eat the roots of grasses and vegetables. Their burrowing can also uproot grasses. Grubs have a strange way of moving around. Their legs are too short to move easily. Instead, they wriggle on their backs. They have ridged backs with short hairs. The hairs help them move through the grasses. Adult June beetles also damage crops. They eat figs and similar fruits.

### FACT BOX

**Range**: Eastern United States
**Habitat**: Soil, short grasses
**Diet**: Fruits as adults, roots and decaying organic matter as grubs

# INSECTS
## GREEN PEACH APHID (MYZUS PERSICAE)

Green peach aphid infestations put stress on plants.

Green peach aphids are tiny, light-green insects. Some have wings, but others do not. Their bodies are shaped like teardrops, and they grow to around 0.07 inches (0.18 cm) long. Despite their small size, they can cause significant damage. They feed primarily on peach trees, but they eat other crops as well, including nectarines and vegetables. Severe infestations can cause crops to fail. Leaves and fruits may grow incorrectly. Fruits may fall off the plant before they are ripe.

Another big problem is that green peach aphids can spread plant diseases. When they feed on plants, they can pass along viruses. These viruses can harm or kill many types of crops, including potatoes and cucumbers.

**FACT BOX**
**Range**: Worldwide
**Habitat**: Plants, such as vegetables and flowers
**Diet**: Leaves, fruits

It is difficult to stop a green peach aphid infestation. These aphids have grown to be resistant to pesticides. The chemicals in pesticides need to be very strong to kill all the aphids. But strong pesticides also damage plants. They can also harm helpful insects and other animals.

Some adult green peach aphids have wings and travel between plants.

## INSECTS
# HERCULES BEETLE *(DYNASTES HERCULES)*

**M**ale and female Hercules beetles look quite different. Males are about 3.3 inches (8.4 cm) long on average. Females are smaller, growing to be around 2.4 inches (6.1 cm) long. They are also different colors. Males range from yellow to black. They are darker when it is more humid. Females are mostly black. But the most noticeable difference between males and females is the horn. A male Hercules beetle has two horns. One emerges from the top of its head. The other grows from its thorax. Females do not have horns.

The horns act like a large claw. Males use their horns to fight each other for mates. A male

The Hercules beetle is one of the largest flying insects in the world.

The Hercules beetle can lift up to 850 times its weight.

Hercules beetle can pick up another male with its horns. It can throw the other beetle to the ground.

Hercules beetles are clumsy fliers. Their large size and bulky horns make it difficult to maneuver. They spend most of their time on the forest floor, where they eat fruits. Scientists have seen these beetles eat for 24 hours straight.

**FACT BOX**
**Range:** Southern North America, Central America, northern South America
**Habitat:** Forests
**Diet:** Rotting fruits as adults, rotting wood as young

# INSECTS
# HONEYBEE (APIS MELLIFERA)

A honeybee is covered in fine hairs.

Honeybees have black and yellow stripes. They have fuzzy heads and bodies. They grow to around 0.6 inches (1.5 cm) long. This honeybee species is also called the western honeybee. These bees are domesticated and raised by beekeepers.

Honeybees are social insects. They live together in colonies. Bees have different jobs. The queen bee produces young. Worker bees care for developing larvae. They also gather food and defend their hive from predators. Workers have stingers with hooks. The hooks make the sting more painful. But honeybees can sting only once. The stinger stays in the victim's body.

Honeybees are important pollinators. They drink nectar from flowers. While they drink, flower pollen sticks to them. They carry the pollen to the next flower they drink from. This helps plants grow and reproduce. Honeybees pollinate 30 percent of the plants eaten in the United States. Honeybees use flower nectar to make honey. They store the nectar in honeycombs. The bees eat the honey during the winter months, when there are fewer flowers.

Beekeepers raise honeybees for their honey production.

But these important insects are in danger. Populations of honeybees suffer from colony collapse disorder. Worker bees suddenly begin to die off. When this happens, the colony's numbers get so low that they can no longer properly care for the queen or the young.

**FACT BOX**

**Range:** Worldwide due to beekeeping and commercial purposes
**Habitat:** Meadows, gardens, wooded areas
**Diet:** Nectar, pollen, honey

# INSECTS
## HOUSEFLY *(MUSCA DOMESTICA)*

Houseflies have big, red eyes and a single pair of wings. They grow to around 0.25 inches (0.6 cm) long. They have small hairs on their bodies that they use to taste.

Females lay eggs in manure piles or garbage. When the eggs hatch, the maggots have easy access to these food sources. Being around so much dirty matter has earned them the nickname filth flies.

A housefly uses its mouthparts to eat food.

Houseflies typically live between 15 and 25 days.

Houseflies have an unusual way of digesting food. For humans, digestion occurs in the body. The stomach has chemicals that break down food. Houseflies, on the other hand, vomit up digestive juices. The chemicals begin to break down the food before houseflies begin eating. They use their mouthparts to drink the digested food. This behavior can spread disease. Houseflies pick up disease-causing germs from manure and garbage. When they land and vomit on food that people eat, they spread germs. People may experience stomach issues after eating this food.

**FACT BOX**

**Range:** Worldwide
**Habitat:** Where people live
**Diet:** Animal feces, garbage

# INSECTS
# HUMMINGBIRD HAWK MOTH (MACROGLOSSUM STELLATARUM)

Hummingbird hawk moths are more active during the day.

The hummingbird hawk moth has a dark-brown back, white belly, and wings in many shades of brown. Its wingspan is about 2.2 inches (5.6 cm). It has a long proboscis. The moth uses this straw-like beak to drink nectar. When not drinking, the proboscis is curled up. It is about 1 inch (2.5 cm) long when unfurled.

The hummingbird hawk moth gets its name for the way it hovers around flowers. Most butterflies and moths flap their wings up and down to fly. Hummingbird hawk moths move their wings like hummingbirds. They flap in a figure eight shape. This creates a pocket of air that supports the moth. They are able to hover in place while drinking nectar. To do this, they beat their wings 85 times per second. These moths can fly at approximately 12 miles per hour (19 kmh).

**FACT BOX**
**Range:** Africa, Asia, Europe
**Habitat:** Fields, urban settings with flowers
**Diet:** Nectar

Hummingbird hawk moths beat their wings so quickly that the movement produces a humming sound.

## INSECTS
# ISABELLA TIGER MOTH (PYRRHARCTIA ISABELLA)

The Isabella tiger moth has tan and orange wings with faint spots. Its wingspan is around 2 inches (5 cm). Like all moth species, the Isabella tiger moth starts off as a caterpillar. It builds a cocoon around itself, where it develops into a moth. The adult Isabella tiger moth has a short life span. It mates and dies within 24 hours.

Lights may attract the Isabella tiger moth at night.

Wooly bear caterpillars are often seen in the fall.

The caterpillar of this species may survive for up to ten years. This is the longest life span of any moth species. The caterpillar is commonly called a wooly bear caterpillar. Its head and rear are black. The middle section is brown or rust colored. The length of the colored section varies among caterpillars. Older caterpillars tend to have a thicker colored band. The wooly bear caterpillar has fuzzy hairs all over its body that secrete a weak venom. These caterpillars are usually harmless to humans, but some people are allergic to wooly bear venom. They may develop a rash after touching a wooly bear.

**FACT BOX**
**Range**: North America
**Habitat**: Forests, meadows
**Diet**: Nothing as adults, plants and leaves as young

## INSECTS
# JAPANESE BEETLE (POPILLIA JAPONICA)

The Japanese beetle has patches of white hair around its abdomen.

The Japanese beetle has a brilliant bright-green head. Its body is a shiny bronze color. It is about 0.5 inches (1.3 cm) long.

Japanese beetles are native to Japan, but they have been in the United States since 1916. They are an invasive species. They cause significant damage in the United States because they do not have natural predators in the country. Adults feed on more than 300 plant species, including roses, apple trees, and soybeans. They eat leaves and flowers. Many plants are able to survive damage from adult Japanese beetles.

Young and unhealthy plants are at greater risk of being killed by these beetles.

Japanese beetle grubs also damage plants. They hatch underground and eat grass roots. This makes it difficult for the grass to get water and nutrients. It begins to die. The grass can easily be pulled out of the ground. Lawns that are infested with grubs may have patchy appearances.

**FACT BOX**

**Range**: Japan, invasive to United States, Canada, and Portugal
**Habitat**: Fields, woods, urban areas
**Diet**: Plants and leaves as adults, grass roots as larvae

Japanese beetles chew holes in leaves and other plant parts.

## INSECTS
# LARGE BLUE CUCKOO WASP (CHRYSIS COERULANS)

The large blue cuckoo wasp is neon blue. Its exoskeleton has many small dents. This gives the insect a shiny appearance. When light strikes the wasp, it glitters like a jewel. The wasp is about 0.5 inches (1.3 cm) long. The wasp has a short stinger. Scientists don't know if the wasp can use its stinger to defend itself.

The large blue cuckoo wasp has a glittery appearance.

Cuckoo wasps were named after the cuckoo bird. This bird lays its eggs in the nests of other bird species. All cuckoo wasp species show the same behavior. Female cuckoo wasps sneak into bee nests or other wasp nests. They lay their eggs inside. Bees and wasps often provide their larvae with food, such as spiders and caterpillars. The cuckoo wasp larvae will eat the food supply. They will also eat the larvae of the other species.

Sometimes the female wasp will get caught sneaking into the nest. She has a way to protect herself. She curls up into a ball. This makes her difficult to sting. The bee or other wasp will carry the cuckoo wasp outside. She will get another chance to sneak inside.

The large blue cuckoo wasp is one of more than 75 cuckoo wasp species.

### FACT BOX
**Range:** Worldwide
**Habitat:** Dry, hot places
**Diet:** Nectar as adults, caterpillars and spiders as young

## INSECTS
# LITTLE BARRIER GIANT WETA *(DEINACRIDA HETERACANTHA)*

The Little Barrier giant weta looks like a huge cricket. This insect is found only on Little Barrier Island in New Zealand. It can grow to more than 4 inches (10 cm) long and weigh up to 2.5 ounces (71 g). This is about as heavy as a songbird. The Little Barrier giant weta has long legs with spines. The spines help it grasp onto the trees it lives in. Its main defense is a hissing noise that it makes by rubbing its leg spines across its body.

Giant wetas blend in with trees.

Weta comes from the Māori word *wetapunga*, which means "god of ugly things."

Some scientists compare giant weta to mice. Both are more active at night. They have similar diets. But giant weta reproduce more slowly. They take a longer time to reach adulthood. Other than a few bat species, there are no mammals native to New Zealand. But rats and mice are now invasive in the country. They outcompete the native giant weta. Giant weta numbers have declined sharply. They are endangered and protected under New Zealand law.

**FACT BOX**

**Range:** New Zealand
**Habitat:** Trees
**Diet:** Leaves

## INSECTS
# LUNA MOTH *(ACTIAS LUNA)*

Luna moths have a wingspan of 4 inches (10 cm). They have feathery antennae. Their wings are always a shade of green, but the color changes depending on when they hatch. Early in spring, the wings are a more vivid green. Luna moths that hatch from their cocoons in the summer have wings that are a yellow-green shade. They have four eye spots on their wings. Their lower wings extend into crescents. Many people consider the luna moth to be one of the most beautiful moth species.

Luna moths dry their wings after emerging from their cocoons.

Luna moth caterpillars may stand on their back legs to scare away predators.

The luna moth caterpillar is bright green with yellow lines and bright-red spots. It also has spiky hairs. The caterpillar spends most of its time eating. This is because the adult moths do not eat. The caterpillar needs to eat a lot so that it has energy to survive as an adult. Luna moth caterpillars primarily eat tree leaves, such as those from birches, oaks, maples, and more.

**FACT BOX**

**Range:** Eastern United States, Canada
**Habitat:** Forested areas
**Diet:** Nothing as adults, leaves as young

# INSECTS
# MILKWEED ASSASSIN BUG (ZELUS LONGIPES)

A milkweed assassin bug catches and eats a fly.

Milkweed assassin bugs are bright orange and black. They have long, spindly legs. They also have long antennae. These insects can grow to be around 0.7 inches (1.8 cm) long.

Assassin bugs are named for the way they hunt. They are ambush predators. They hide until prey comes along. Then they jump out and strike. The bugs' legs are covered in a sticky substance that helps them trap their prey. They eat many types of insects, including mosquitoes, aphids, and caterpillars. Milkweed assassin bugs bite into their prey. Their saliva has chemicals that paralyze prey. It also has digestive juices. These juices cause the prey's insides to break down into liquid. The milkweed assassin bug can then drink the prey.

Milkweed assassin bugs are helpful for gardeners and farmers. They eat many insects, including pests that destroy plants. However, they may bite humans in defense. This causes a sharp, stinging feeling.

## FACT BOX
**Range:** North America, South America, West Indies
**Habitat:** Gardens, fields
**Diet:** Insects

Milkweed assassin bugs have white markings on the edges of their abdomens.

# INSECTS
# MONARCH BUTTERFLY (DANAUS PLEXIPPUS)

Monarch butterflies have 3-to-4-inch (7.6 to 10 cm) wingspans. Their wings are mostly orange with black lines and white spots. In the spring and summer months, monarchs can be found all over the United States and Canada. But as the weather turns cold, monarchs migrate. They are one of the only insects to do this. Some monarchs winter in southern California. Others fly all the way to Mexico. The migratory route can be more than 3,000 miles (4,830 km). Monarchs head back north when the weather warms.

Monarch butterflies live for about four to five weeks.

Tens of thousands of monarch butterflies can gather in a single tree, clustering together for warmth.

Monarch butterflies lay their eggs on milkweed plants. Monarch caterpillars eat only this plant. The caterpillars have yellow, black, and white stripes. They have a pair of tentacles on the front and rear.

Monarch butterfly populations have decreased dramatically in recent years. Monarch butterfly numbers in the eastern United States have declined by more than 80 percent over the past 20 years. These butterflies are threatened by habitat loss and climate change.

### FACT BOX

**Range:** North America, South America, Australia, Pacific Islands
**Habitat:** Forests, fields, mountains
**Diet:** Nectar as adults, milkweed as young

# INSECTS
# NORTHERN MOLE CRICKET (NEOCURTILLA HEXADACTYLA)

The northern mole cricket has strong hind legs that help it jump far distances.

The northern mole cricket has a dark-brown body. It grows to 1.5 inches (3.8 cm) long and has a large head. This cricket has tiny hairs along its body. These hairs help prevent soil from sticking to the insect. The northern mole cricket's forelegs set it apart from other cricket species. They end in hand-like structures. They look like mole paws. Similar to moles, these crickets spend a lot of time digging. They burrow just beneath the surface in search of food, such as earthworms. Their tunneling can damage grass roots. Females also lay their eggs in their burrows.

## FACT BOX
**Range**: North America
**Habitat**: Underground
**Diet**: Earthworms

The northern mole cricket is more active at night, when it may come to the surface. It can dig 20 feet (6.1 m) in a single night. The cricket travels mainly by running and flying.

A northern mole cricket digs through the sand.

# INSECTS
# NORTHERN WALKING STICK (DIAPHEROMERA FEMORATA)

Northern walking sticks look like sticks. Males are completely brown and grow to 2.9 inches (7.4 cm) long. Females have a bit of green coloration and grow slightly larger, around 3.7 inches (9.4 cm) long. These walking sticks have long, skinny legs. They also have very long antennae that are about two-thirds the length of their bodies.

Their appearance serves as camouflage. These insects spend most

Northern walking sticks are able to regrow their legs if they lose one to a predator.

Camouflage protects northern walking sticks from predators.

of their time in trees. They blend in easily with the branches. They may sway their bodies when there is a breeze. This makes them look like twigs shaking in the wind.

Northern walking sticks eat tree leaves. They prefer oak and hazelnut leaves, but they are known to eat other leaves as well. Large populations of these insects can harm trees. They may eat so much that tree branches die. Typically, predators such as birds keep this walking stick's numbers balanced.

**FACT BOX**
**Range:** North America
**Habitat:** Forests
**Diet:** Leaves, flowers

# INSECTS
# ORCHID MANTIS (HYMENOPUS CORONATUS)

An orchid mantis stays very still as it waits for prey to come close.

**M**ale and female orchid mantises have very different appearances. The male is a greenish-brown color. It grows to be about 1 inch (2.5 cm) long. Females are much larger. They can be more than 2.5 inches (6.3 cm) long. They also have more vibrant colors. They may be white, yellow, or pink. They have petal-like legs and look like flowers.

Along with different appearances, male and female orchid mantises have different behaviors. Males hide from predators. They use their small size to ambush prey. Males also sneak up on females to mate. Like other mantis species, females may kill males that try to mate with them. Females use their flower-like appearance to attract pollinators. They are the first animal known to mimic flowers. Their disguise is so convincing that pollinators will investigate the mantis even when it is not hiding among other flowers. When the pollinator flies close, the female orchid mantis will strike. The camouflage also helps the mantis hide from predators.

**FACT BOX**
**Range:** Southeast Asia
**Habitat:** Rain forests
**Diet:** Small insects

The hind legs of an orchid mantis have a petal-like shape.

# INSECTS
# PAINTED GRASSHOPPER *(DACTYLOTUM BICOLOR)*

The painted grasshopper is known for its striking colors.

Painted grasshoppers are brilliantly colored. They have bands of red, orange, blue, black, and white stripes. They are sometimes called rainbow grasshoppers because of their many colors. Painted grasshoppers, like many brightly colored animals, are poisonous. The colorful stripes of the painted grasshopper warn predators that the grasshopper is harmful to eat. The painted grasshopper has short wings. It cannot fly. It grows to around 1.4 inches (3.5 cm) long.

Painted grasshoppers do not typically gather in large groups. They feed on grasses and weeds such as dandelions.

Because there are not large swarms of painted grasshoppers, the species is not considered a threat to crops.

**FACT BOX**
**Range:** North America
**Habitat:** Short grasses
**Diet:** Grasses, plants

Painted grasshoppers primarily feed on grasses.

# INSECTS
# PHARAOH CICADA (MAGICICADA SEPTENDECIM)

Pharaoh cicadas have black bodies. They have striking red eyes and legs. Their wings are clear with orange veins. They are about 1.5 inches (3.8 cm) long when full-grown.

A generation of cicadas is called a brood. A brood may contain billions of individuals. They all emerge at the same time. Their overwhelming numbers are a form of protection.

A large brood of pharaoh cicadas can make a sound as loud as a motorcycle.

A female pharaoh cicada lays approximately 500 eggs.

Predators cannot eat all of them. Pharaoh cicadas have a 17-year life cycle. They usually lay their eggs in trees. When the eggs hatch, the young pharaoh cicadas spend a short amount of time above ground. Then they burrow underground, where they remain for many years. They suck fluids from tree roots.

All cicada species are known for their songs. Only male cicadas produce songs. The song is part of the mating process. Each cicada species has a different mating call.

**FACT BOX**
**Range:** Midwest and eastern United States
**Habitat:** Underground as young, near trees as adults
**Diet:** Sap

## INSECTS
# RAINBOW SCARAB BEETLE (PHANAEUS VINDEX)

Rainbow scarab beetles have glittery exoskeletons.

Rainbow scarab beetles have brightly colored green and bronze shells. Their shells look shiny. They grow to around 0.8 inches (2 cm) long. Male rainbow scarab beetles have a horn on their heads.

These beetles are part of the dung beetle family. Dung is animal waste. It is an important part of the rainbow scarab's diet and lifestyle. A female rainbow scarab beetle will gather dung. She begins rolling it. This action shapes the dung into a rounded structure called a brood ball. This action also attracts the attention of a male. He will help her roll the dung and create a burrow. They place the brood ball on top of the burrow entrance. The female will lay her eggs on the brood ball. When the larvae hatch, they eat the dung.

Rainbow scarab beetles burrow underground to breed.

Dung beetles such as the rainbow scarab beetle play important roles in their ecosystems. They digest dung. This helps nutrients return to the soil.

**FACT BOX**
**Range:** Eastern United States
**Habitat:** Pastures
**Diet:** Animal dung

## INSECTS
# REGAL MOTH (CITHERONIA REGALIS)

Hickory horned devils are among the largest caterpillars.

Regal moths have gray wings with orange stripes and yellow spots. These moths grow to be quite large. They can have a wingspan of 6 inches (15 cm). They have small mouths and cannot eat as adults. Regal moths have long, feathery antennae. They use their antennae to smell. Females have a certain scent. Males fly toward the smell in order to find a mate.

Regal moth caterpillars are called hickory horned devils. They are typically a blue-green color. They are covered in black spikes. They have several orange spikes on their heads. Hickory horned devils can grow to be 5.5 inches (14 cm) long. Despite their appearances, they are harmless creatures.

The caterpillars feed on a variety of trees and plants. They are commonly found on hickory trees. They also eat walnut and sycamore leaves.

**FACT BOX**
**Range:** Eastern and southern United States
**Habitat:** Woodlands
**Diet:** Nothing as adults, leaves as young

Adult regal moths typically do not live for more than two weeks.

115

# INSECTS
# ROSEMARY BEETLE (CHRYSOLINA AMERICANA)

The rosemary beetle is known for its beautiful colors. These beetles have shiny, dark-green abdomens with purple stripes. They are small bugs. They grow to be approximately 0.25 inches (0.6 cm) long.

Rosemary beetles are commonly found on rosemary plants. They also eat other fragrant plants such as lavender and thyme. These beetles are found in Europe. Since the 1990s, they have

Rosemary beetles have a colorful, metallic appearance.

Rosemary beetles feed on rosemary and other plants.

become widespread in the United Kingdom, where they are considered pests. They eat the leaves and flowers of plants. In small numbers, rosemary beetles do not eat enough to cause significant damage to plants.

Rosemary beetles lay their eggs under rosemary leaves. Larvae eat the plant. Then they burrow into the soil, where they continue to develop. After about two weeks, they emerge from the soil as adult beetles.

**FACT BOX**
**Range:** Europe
**Habitat:** Gardens
**Diet:** Herbs, such as rosemary and thyme

# INSECTS
# ROSY MAPLE MOTH (DRYOCAMPA RUBICUNDA)

Rosy maple moth caterpillars are called green striped mapleworms.

The rosy maple moth has fuzzy wings with brightly colored pink and yellow bands. It has a wingspan of about 2 inches (5 cm). Males are typically smaller than females. The males have long, fuzzy antennae. They use their antennae to smell. The female moths release chemical scents called pheromones. The scents signal that she is ready to mate.

Rosy maple moth caterpillars also have striking appearances. They are bright-green with black spots. They have white stripes that run along their bodies. The caterpillars have long, black antennae. They have a red patch near their rears.

Maple trees are a favorite food of rosy maple moth caterpillars. They also feed on oak trees. The caterpillars do not typically cause lasting damage to the trees. But their feeding is more harmful to young trees and trees that were already unhealthy.

**FACT BOX**

**Range:** North America
**Habitat:** Forests
**Diet:** Nothing as adults, trees and leaves as young

Rosy maple moth wings come in many shades of pink and cream.

## INSECTS
# SADDLEBACK CATERPILLAR MOTH (ACHARIA STIMULEA)

The saddleback caterpillar moth has dark-brown wings. It can have a wingspan of 1.7 inches (4.3 cm). Females are typically larger than males. They lay their eggs on plant leaves. The eggs are clustered together and often overlap.

While the adult saddleback caterpillar moth has a plain appearance, the caterpillar is much more colorful. Its head and

The saddleback caterpillar moth is more commonly seen during the summer months.

The saddleback caterpillar eats many types of plants.

rear are brown. Its body is green. It has a single brown spot on its back. The spot looks like a saddle. The bright coloring shows that the caterpillar is poisonous. It has knobs that grow around its body. It also has a pair of horns on top of its head and rear. The knobs and horns are covered in small spines. The spines contain venom. The caterpillars sting predators that get too close.

**FACT BOX**

**Range:** Eastern United States
**Habitat:** Forests
**Diet:** Nothing as adults, leaves as young

## INSECTS
# SEVEN-SPOTTED LADYBIRD (COCCINELLA SEPTEMPUNCTATA)

Seven-spotted ladybirds have bright-red shells with exactly seven black spots. The bright-red color signals to predators that the ladybirds do not taste good. Their thoraxes are black with white markings. Seven-spotted ladybirds are small and grow only to about 0.3 inches (0.8 cm) long. Other ladybird species have a different number of spots. Ladybirds are also called ladybugs.

The seven-spotted ladybird helps gardeners by eating aphids.

There are approximately 5,000 ladybird species in the world.

Ladybirds are a type of beetle. Like all beetles, they start out as grubs. All ladybird grubs look similar to caterpillars. They have long, black bodies with orange spots. Grubs undergo many changes as they develop.

Adult ladybirds and ladybird grubs mostly eat aphids. Aphids drink plant sap, which harms plants. Ladybirds help control these pests. They can eat more than 5,000 aphids during their lifetimes.

**FACT BOX**
**Range:** Worldwide
**Habitat:** Woods, gardens
**Diet:** Aphids

## INSECTS
# SILVERFISH (LEPISMA SACCHARINA)

Silverfish cause damage to books.

Silverfish get their name for their silver color. They have flat bodies, which allow them to slip between small cracks. They can grow to around 0.75 inches (1.9 cm) long. Silverfish have two pale antennae on their heads. They also have three tail-like structures that extend from their rears. They can regrow their antennae and tail structures in about four weeks. They can live for up to eight years.

Silverfish typically live in cool, damp places. They can be found under rocks and in caves. They are pests that may infest buildings. They can thrive in basements and attics. Silverfish eat dust and dead insects. They also eat wood and paper products. They are known to eat books. But they also have an appetite for fabrics, cereals, and other insects.

**FACT BOX**
**Range:** Worldwide
**Habitat:** Cool, damp areas
**Diet:** Mostly wood, paper products

Silverfish run quickly to escape predators.

# INSECTS
# SOUTHERN FLANNEL MOTH (MEGALOPYGE OPERCULARIS)

Southern flannel moths are covered with soft, yellow hairs. Their yellow wings have a black edge near the top. Their wingspans can reach 1.5 inches (3.8 cm). Males have longer antennae than females.

The southern flannel moth caterpillar is known as a puss caterpillar. It looks like a cat's tail. Similar to the adult moths, the caterpillars are covered in hair. They have thick, brown coats. But the caterpillars' hairs contain venom. When the hairs are broken, they inject the venom. Puss caterpillars are one of the most venomous caterpillars in the United States. Their venom causes pain and swelling, but it is not strong enough to kill humans.

The southern flannel moth can be identified by its furry appearance.

Older puss caterpillars are more venomous than younger puss caterpillars.

Puss caterpillars make cocoons. They enter these structures to develop into moths. The cocoons are very strong. Ants and spiders have been seen using empty cocoons for shelter.

### FACT BOX

**Range:** Eastern United States
**Habitat:** Trees, such as oak and elm
**Diet:** Leaves

## INSECTS
# TARANTULA HAWK (PEPSIS THISBE)

Adult tarantula hawks drink only nectar.

The tarantula hawk is a type of wasp. It has a metallic blue body and orange wings. It can grow up to 2 inches (5 cm) in length. The female wasps have long stingers that can be up to 0.25 inches (0.6 cm) long. The males do not have stingers. The tarantula hawk has one of the most painful stings of all insects, but the pain does not last long. A person typically recovers after five minutes.

The tarantula hawk is named for the prey it feeds to its young. The female wasps hunt tarantulas. They attack and sting the large spiders. The venom in their stings paralyzes the tarantulas. The wasp lays an egg inside the spider. The tarantula is still alive when the egg hatches. The larva eats the tarantula. It avoids eating important organs so that the spider is kept alive for as long as possible.

**FACT BOX**
**Range:** Southwestern United States, Central America, South America
**Habitat:** Deserts, dry places
**Diet:** Nectar as adults, tarantulas and other large bugs as young

A female tarantula hawk drags a tarantula back to her burrow.

# INSECTS
## THORN BUG *(UMBONIA CRASSICORNIS)*

Thorn bugs are named for their shape. They look like the thorns found on plants such as roses. The thorn structure on these bugs varies between individuals. Some have larger thorns than others. The thorns may appear flatter on some thorn bugs. These insects are mostly green. They may also have yellow, red, or brown markings along the thorn. On average, adults are 0.5 inches (1.3 cm) long.

A thorn bug's camouflage makes it difficult to spot.

The thorn gives the bug many advantages. It can blend in with plants. Predators may stay away from the pointy bug. Thorn bugs use their sharp beaks to pierce holes in plants. They suck sap. They also lay their eggs within plants. This can harm plants. They may lose leaves and branches.

Female thorn bugs care for their young. They guard their eggs and continue to protect the young once they hatch. Because of this, about 50 percent of thorn bugs survive into adulthood.

## FACT BOX

**Range:** South and Central America, Mexico, Florida
**Habitat:** Trees, bushes
**Diet:** Sap

An infestation of thorn bugs clusters together.

# INSECTS
# YELLOW FEVER MOSQUITO *(AEDES AEGYPTI)*

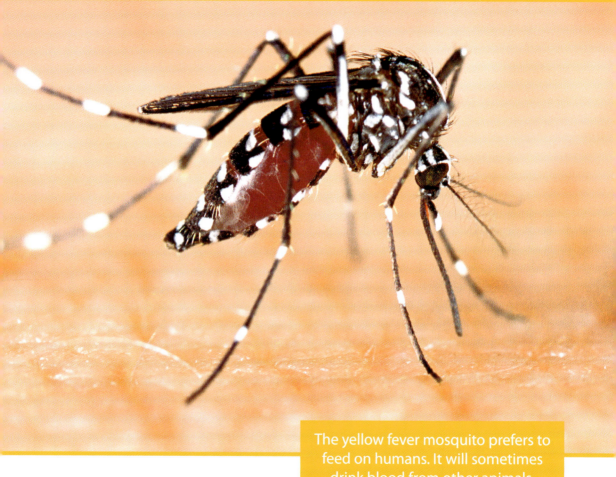

The yellow fever mosquito prefers to feed on humans. It will sometimes drink blood from other animals.

The yellow fever mosquito is black and white. It has long legs and fuzzy antennae. It is about 0.25 inches (0.6 cm) long when fully grown.

All mosquito species drink nectar and blood. However, only female mosquitoes have the mouthparts to drink blood. They need to consume blood in order to reproduce. The more blood a female drinks, the more eggs she can lay. Mosquitoes lay their eggs in slow-moving or still water, such as a clogged gutter.

Mosquito larvae eat organic matter such as algae.

Mosquitoes are more active in the summer months. People are more likely to get bitten during this time. Mosquito bites may be itchy for several days. Mosquitoes can also carry disease. They infect humans while they drink blood. They can transmit diseases such as yellow fever and Zika. These diseases can be very severe or even deadly.

## FACT BOX

**Range:** Africa, tropical areas of North America, Central America, South America
**Habitat:** Trees, plants
**Diet:** Blood and nectar as adults, organic matter as young

Yellow fever mosquitoes can be found on nectar-producing plants.

## ARACHNIDS
# BIRD DUNG CRAB SPIDER (PHRYNARACHNE CEYLONICA)

Female bird dung crab spiders grow to be around 0.4 inches (1 cm) long. Male bird dung crab spiders tend to be much smaller than females. The bird dung crab spider is typically black and white. It may also appear yellow or brown. It has lumps on its abdomen. It has the appearance of bird poop. In addition to the coloring, the spider also has a foul smell. This makes its disguise even more convincing.

A bird dung crab spider captures a fly.

Bird dung crab spiders ambush their prey.

Its camouflage protects the bird dung crab spider from predators. Predators such as birds are unlikely to show interest in something that looks and smells like poop. However, insects such as flies eat poop. A fly may approach the bird dung crab spider. It thinks the spider is food. When the fly gets near, the bird dung crab spider attacks. The fly is eaten instead. The bird dung crab spider may sit on a leaf for hours. It stays still to appear as similar as possible to bird poop.

### FACT BOX

**Range:** Southeast Asia
**Habitat:** Forests
**Diet:** Insects, such as flies

## ARACHNIDS
# BLACK-LEGGED TICK *(IXODES SCAPULARIS)*

Black-legged ticks live for about two years.

The black-legged tick has a teardrop-shaped body. Adults are typically 0.13 inches (0.3 cm) long. They can grow to be around 0.5 inches (1.3 cm) long after feeding. They are similar in size and shape to sesame seeds. Males are all brown, but females have an orangish body.

All tick species have three life stages. They start off as larvae. Then they molt and develop into nymphs. They molt again and become full-grown adults. Ticks drink blood throughout their lives. They will have one blood meal during each life stage. Without blood, the tick does not have enough energy to molt or reproduce. They eat slowly. They may feed on the host animal for up to five days.

Black-legged ticks are also called deer ticks. This is because the adult ticks are often found on large mammals such as deer. They can be found on other animals and on humans too. Nymphs also may feed on people. Most tick bites are harmless. But black-legged ticks are known for carrying bacteria that cause Lyme disease. An infected tick must feed on a person for at least 36 hours to pass along the bacteria.

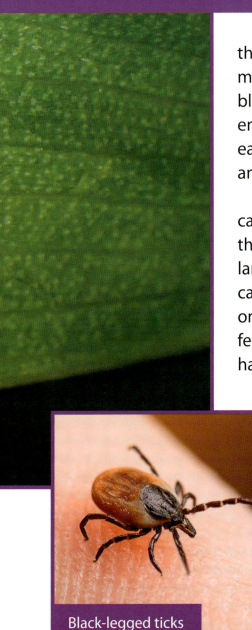

Black-legged ticks can spread diseases as they drink blood from a person.

## FACT BOX

**Range:** Eastern half of North America
**Habitat:** Forests, long grasses
**Diet:** Blood

## ARACHNIDS
# BRAZILIAN BLACK TARANTULA (GRAMMOSTOLA PULCHRA)

The Brazilian black tarantula is covered in black hairs. It has a velvety appearance. It is about 8 inches (20 cm) long when fully grown. Males are typically smaller than females but have longer legs. Males also have shorter life spans than females. They live for about seven years. Females may live for more than 20 years.

Brazilian black tarantulas are known to eat each other.

A Brazilian black tarantula eats a grasshopper.

The hairs that cover the Brazilian black tarantula help the spider sense movement. They also protect the spider. The tarantula can use its legs to flick hairs off its body. The hairs have small hooks at the end. They can be harmful to predators.

The Brazilian black tarantula makes burrows. It will wait near the entrance of the burrow. When prey such as a cricket comes close, the tarantula attacks. A male will enter a female's burrow when it is time to mate. A female can lay more than 600 eggs at a time. She guards them until they hatch.

**FACT BOX**
**Range**: Brazil, Uruguay
**Habitat**: Grasslands, underground
**Diet**: Mice, lizards, crickets

## ARACHNIDS
# BROWN RECLUSE SPIDER (LOXOSCELES RECLUSA)

Brown recluse spiders have three pairs of eyes.

Brown recluse spiders have brown bodies and legs. They have a violin-shaped marking on their heads and thoraxes. They have six eyes that form a semicircle on the front of their heads. Females are larger than males. Female brown recluses can grow to be around 0.25 inches (0.6 cm) long.

Like most spiders, brown recluse spiders are shy and prefer to stay away from humans. They eat insects such as crickets and cockroaches. They are often found in undisturbed areas, such as under rocks. They can also be found indoors in places such as closets and basements. Brown recluses can get rid of insect pests, but they can be dangerous. They have a venomous bite. The bite may not be painful at first but can become serious over time. The bite site becomes red and swollen. The venom can cause skin tissue to die. People should seek medical attention if they think they have been bitten by a brown recluse.

**FACT BOX**

**Range:** South-central United States
**Habitat:** Dark, undisturbed areas
**Diet:** Insects, other spiders

Brown recluse spiders are about the size of a quarter.

## ARACHNIDS
# CAMEL SPIDER (GALEODES ARABS)

The camel spider is tan with a black abdomen. In addition to its eight legs, the camel spider has two other leg-like structures. They help the arachnid sense its surroundings. The camel spider can grow quite large. It is about 6 inches (15 cm) long when fully grown. The camel spider lives in the desert. It is also known as a wind scorpion. Despite its name, it is neither a spider nor a scorpion. It is a different type of arachnid known as a solpugid.

Camel spiders are more active at night.

Camel spiders are fierce predators. They can run up to 10 miles per hour (16 kmh). Their jaws make up a third of their body length. They use their jaws to catch prey and inject digestive juices. Then they can suck up the prey's insides. The camel spider eats insects and small creatures such as rodents, lizards, and small birds. Its bite is painful but not deadly to humans.

## FACT BOX

**Range**: Middle East
**Habitat**: Deserts
**Diet**: Insects, lizards, rodents, small birds

Some camel spiders produce hissing sounds.

# ARACHNIDS
## DADDY LONGLEGS *(PHOLCUS PHALANGIOIDES)*

Daddy longlegs often make horizontal webs.

The name *daddy longlegs* is used to describe many arthropod species. They are named for their long legs. The daddy longlegs spider is also called the longbodied cellar spider. It has long, spindly legs that are nearly transparent. It has a pale-brown body that is usually around 0.25 inches (0.6 cm) long. But the legs can be around 1.9 inches (4.8 cm) long.

Daddy longlegs are found in dark, undisturbed places. They live in caves. They also are commonly found in basements and garages. These spiders eat other insects and can limit the numbers of household pests.

These spiders build irregularly shaped webs to catch food. A daddy longlegs may enter the web of another daddy longlegs. It kills the web's owner and uses the web for itself. If the web is disturbed, the daddy longlegs moves in a circle. This makes the spider difficult to see.

### FACT BOX
**Range:** Worldwide
**Habitat:** Dark areas, such as caves or basements
**Diet:** Spiders, insects

Female daddy longlegs will protect their eggs until they hatch.

# ARACHNIDS
# DEATHSTALKER SCORPION *(LAURUS QUINQUESTRIATUS)*

Deathstalker scorpions grow to around 4 inches (10 cm) long. They are mostly yellow with darker abdomens. Their legs, heads, and tails are lighter in color. Their tails end in a stinger.

Deathstalker scorpions do not have strong eyesight. They rely on other senses to hunt. They have sensory organs on their

Deathstalker scorpions live in dry, rocky habitats.

Deathstalker scorpions have to watch out for bats that want to prey on them. Some bats have a resistance to the scorpion's venom.

legs that can detect vibrations. The vibrations let the scorpions know where prey is located. Then they can strike quickly with their tails. They can move their tails nearly 3 miles per hour (4.8 kmh). The venom in their tails is very strong. It can cause paralysis and other symptoms. Deathstalker scorpions are considered one of the deadliest scorpion species. People may die if stung.

Scientists are studying deathstalker scorpion venom. They believe that it can have health benefits if used correctly. It may be used to treat cancer in the future.

**FACT BOX**
**Range**: Middle East, North Africa
**Habitat**: Deserts
**Diet**: Insects

## ARACHNIDS
# EMPEROR SCORPION (PANDINUS IMPERATOR)

The emperor scorpion is one of the largest scorpion species in the world. Emperor scorpions grow to around 7.8 inches (19.8 cm) long. They have shiny, black bodies. They are able to detect vibrations using special organs on their legs. Like all scorpions, emperor scorpions have stingers with venom. But their venom is mild in comparison to other scorpion species. The sting is about as painful as a bee sting to people. However,

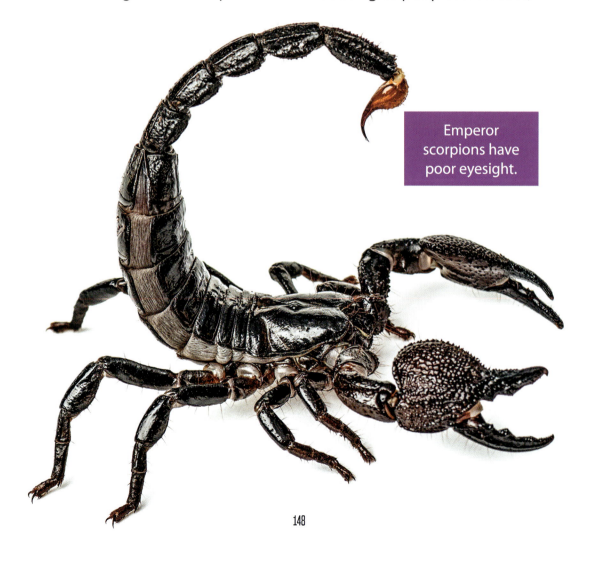

Emperor scorpions have poor eyesight.

Young emperor scorpions are much lighter in color than adults.

it is deadly to small insects. Emperor scorpions mainly use their stingers to defend themselves. They rely on their large claws to hunt prey.

Emperor scorpions are more active at night. A dozen or more of these scorpions may live together in burrows. All scorpion species give birth to live young. The young scorpions are defenseless. The female carries the baby scorpions on her back until they are able to take care of themselves.

### FACT BOX
**Range:** West Africa
**Habitat:** Forests
**Diet:** Insects

## ARACHNIDS
# GIANT HUNTSMAN SPIDER (HETEROPODA MAXIMA)

Giant huntsman spiders are black and brown. They have some of the longest legs of any spider species. Their legs can span 12 inches (30 cm) in length. Their outstretched legs make them look like crabs. Similar to crabs, their legs have joints that allow them to crawl sideways. These spiders can grow to be the size of dinner plates. Males are smaller than females but tend to have longer legs.

The giant huntsman spider, like other huntsman spider species, has eight eyes.

A giant huntsman spider can squeeze through small openings to enter homes.

Giant huntsman spiders eat cockroaches and other household pests. They chase after and hunt down their prey. They inject their prey with venom. These spiders are not usually aggressive toward humans. A person who is bitten by a giant huntsman spider experiences only mild symptoms. A female is most likely to attack when she is guarding her eggs. She lays approximately 200 eggs at a time. She watches over them until they hatch, which takes about three weeks. She does not eat during this time.

**FACT BOX**
**Range**: Australia
**Habitat**: Under tree bark or rocks
**Diet**: Insects, spiders

## ARACHNIDS
# GIANT WHIP SCORPION (MASTIGOPROCTUS GIGANTEUS)

Giant whip scorpions are more closely related to spiders than scorpions.

The giant whip scorpion has a black body and massive front claws. It can grow up to 3 inches (7.6 cm) long. This arachnid has a long, thin tail that does not have a stinger. The tail has sensory organs that help the whip scorpion learn about its surroundings. Despite its name, the giant whip scorpion is not a type of scorpion. It belongs to a group of arachnids called Thelyphonida.

The giant whip scorpion does not have any venom. Even though its tail does not have a stinger, it still warns predators to stay away. It produces a chemical that can burn skin. The chemical smells like vinegar. Because of this, the giant whip scorpion is also called a vinegaroon.

Giant whip scorpions also have powerful claws that they use to rip apart prey. Their claws can be painful to humans. Males have larger claws than females.

### FACT BOX

**Range:** Southern United States, Mexico
**Habitat:** Dark places, under rotting logs, in burrows
**Diet:** Termites, cockroaches, crickets

Giant whip scorpions have large pincers that they use to crush prey.

# ARACHNIDS
# GOLDENROD CRAB SPIDER (MISUMENA VATIA)

A goldenrod crab spider feeds on a fly.

The goldenrod crab spider is typically yellow or white. It can change its color to blend into its surroundings. However, this process can take several days. Females and males of this species have a different appearance. Females may have a reddish-orange stripe along either side of their abdomens. They have light-colored legs. Males are solid in color and may look slightly green. Their legs are a dark purple. Females are also larger than males. Females can grow to be more than 0.25 inches (0.6 cm) long. Males do not typically grow more than 0.13 inches (0.3 cm) in length.

Goldenrod crab spiders do not spin webs. They wait in the centers of flowers for pollinators to fly close. They often sit in goldenrod flowers that match their yellow bodies. They grab insects with their front legs when they fly nearby. Their front legs are very powerful. A goldenrod spider is able to take down prey that is larger than itself.

**FACT BOX**
**Range:** North America, Europe
**Habitat:** Flowers
**Diet:** Insects

A goldenrod crab spider's colors help it blend in with its surroundings.

## ARACHNIDS
# GOLIATH BIRD SPIDER (THERAPHOSA BLONDI)

Goliath bird spiders are black or brown. They are a type of tarantula and have hairy bodies. Goliath bird spiders are one of the biggest spiders in the world. They have a leg span of up to 12 inches (30 cm). They can weigh up to 6 ounces (170 g).

The goliath bird spider is large enough to catch and eat small birds. However, birds are not its prey of choice. The spider more commonly eats insects, small rodents, and toads. They pounce on and bite their prey, injecting them with venom. Their venom is strong enough to kill small creatures.

The goliath bird spider is large enough to kill mice.

A goliath bird spider raises its front legs to show off its large fangs.

The goliath bird spider drags the prey back to its web-lined burrow to drink its insides.

These spiders can defend themselves against predators. They make a loud hissing noise as a warning. They can also fling hairs at predators. Their hairs have barbs at the end that are painful if they land on the target.

### FACT BOX

**Range:** South America
**Habitat:** Underground in rain forests
**Diet:** Insects, frogs, mice, occasionally birds

# ARACHNIDS
# INDIAN RED SCORPION (HOTTENTOTTA TAMULUS)

The Indian red scorpion has a red-orange body. Like other scorpions, it has long pincers and a venomous stinger. It can grow to be 3.5 inches (8.9 cm) long.

These scorpions are nocturnal. This means they are more active at night. They can sense vibrations through the ground and air. This helps them track down their prey. Indian red scorpions ambush and sting their prey. They eat cockroaches and other insects. They also hunt small creatures such as rodents and lizards.

An Indian red scorpion rests with its recent molt, *right*.

Scientists study Indian red scorpion venom for use in medicines.

An Indian red scorpion may also sting in self-defense. It is considered to be one of the deadliest scorpions in the world. Its venom is strong enough to cause paralysis and heart failure in humans. People can die after getting stung by this scorpion.

## FACT BOX

**Range:** India, Pakistan, Sri Lanka, Nepal
**Habitat:** Humid places, human houses
**Diet:** Insects, small animals

## ARACHNIDS
# MEXICAN RED KNEE TARANTULA (BRACHYPELMA HAMORII)

**M**exican red knee tarantulas are mostly black. They have hairy bodies and rust-red stripes that cover their legs and part of their backs. They grow to be around 5 inches (12.7 cm) long.

These tarantulas are ambush predators. They live in underground burrows that they line with spider silk. They also

Some people keep Mexican red knee tarantulas as pets.

Mexican red knee tarantulas have two sensory structures near their heads.

put silk at the opening of their burrows. The silk vibrates when disturbed. If prey walks over the silk, the tarantula feels vibrations through the silk. Then the tarantula can dart out and grab its prey. It uses its venomous fangs to bite into prey. The venom is strong enough to kill small animals, but it is not deadly to humans.

A female Mexican red knee tarantula may lay 400 eggs at once. She wraps the eggs in silk, forming an egg sac. She carries the egg sac in her fangs. Young tarantulas hatch from their eggs after about three months. They do not leave the egg sac for another three weeks.

**FACT BOX**
**Range:** Mexico
**Habitat:** Deserts, forests
**Diet:** Insects, frogs, mice

# ARACHNIDS
# PEACOCK SPIDER (MARATUS VOLANS)

Female and male peacock spiders have different appearances. Females are mostly brown. Males are more vibrantly colored. Their abdomens are mostly yellow with streaks of blue, orange, and green. This flashy appearance is part of the reason for their name. These spiders are very small. They grow to be only about 0.2 inches (0.5 cm) long.

Males use their bright colors to impress females. They have elaborate mating rituals. Males will climb to a high surface. They raise their third pair of legs above their bodies.

Peacock spiders will eat any insect they can grab.

The *Maratus jacatus* is another peacock spider species known for its mating dance.

They also lift their abdomens in the air. Their abdomens have flaps. They fan open these flaps like a peacock. This widens the colorful display. Males then move their abdomens in a circle, dancing to impress females. They may continue to dance for 50 minutes. If the female is not interested in mating, she may eat the male.

**FACT BOX**
**Range:** Australia
**Habitat:** Wetlands
**Diet:** Insects

## ARACHNIDS
# PEACOCK TARANTULA *(POECILOTHERIA METALLICA)*

Female peacock tarantulas have a longer life span than males.

P eacock tarantulas have bluish-gray bodies. Their long, blue legs have white and yellow markings. Young peacock tarantulas may appear lavender in color. Males of this species tend to have more vibrant colors than females.

The peacock tarantula spends most of its time in trees. It hides in holes in the bark and waits for prey to pass by. It snatches flying insects out of the air with its long legs. Then it bites into the prey and injects it with venom. Its venom is powerful. If the tarantula bites a person, he or she may experience a racing heartbeat, headache, and other symptoms. These symptoms can last for a week.

Peacock tarantulas are critically endangered. They are found only in 39 square miles (101 sq km) of forest in India and Sri Lanka. Their habitat is being destroyed by deforestation. People also catch and sell these tarantulas as pets, reducing their numbers even more.

**FACT BOX**
**Range**: India, Sri Lanka
**Habitat**: Trees
**Diet**: Large insects, small rodents

Peacock tarantulas are also called metallic tarantulas.

## ARACHNIDS
# TWO-SPOTTED SPIDER MITE (TETRANYCHUS URTICAE)

Two-spotted spider mites have yellow-orange bodies. They have a dark spot on each side of their abdomens. They are sometimes transparent in appearance. These arachnids are very tiny. They are only 0.02 inches (0.05 cm) long.

These mites are best known for being pests. They suck the sap out of leaves. Leaves that do not have enough sap turn

It can be difficult to see a two-spotted spider mite without a magnification device.

Plants infested with two-spotted spider mites are covered with webbing.

brown and die. Two-spotted spider mites can feed on hundreds of plant species. They have been found on many kinds of fruits, vegetables, trees, and flowers. Severe infestations cause the plant to die. Plants that were already unhealthy are most likely to be infested. Gardeners can look for signs of these spider mites. At early stages of infestation, leaves may have a spotted appearance. Even though they are not spiders, spider mites produce webbing. This webbing is a sign of an infestation of these mites.

**FACT BOX**

**Range:** United States, Europe
**Habitat:** Forests
**Diet:** Leaves, plants

# ARACHNIDS
# WESTERN BLACK WIDOW *(LATRODECTUS HESPERUS)*

The red marking on a spider's abdomen makes it easily identifiable as a black widow species.

Female western black widow spiders have glossy black bodies. They have a red or orange hourglass marking on their round abdomens. Females can grow to be more than 0.25 inches (0.6 cm) long. Male black widows look different. They tend to be brown or gray. The hourglass marking is not as vibrant and is yellow or orange. Males are also much smaller than females. They are about one-third the size of females.

Black widow venom is 15 times stronger than rattlesnake venom. But the spider's bite is less likely to be fatal. Only small amounts of venom are injected at a time. Black widows do not often bite people, but bites can be serious. A person who has been bitten by a black widow should seek medical attention.

Black widow spiders often spin webs in dark, undisturbed places. They can be found under woodpiles and in shrubs. They may also spin webs in the corners of basements. Male and female black widow spiders may share webs. Under extreme conditions, females may eat males. But this behavior is rare.

### FACT BOX
**Range:** Southwestern United States
**Habitat:** Deserts, dry and warm areas
**Diet:** Insects

A western black widow captures a grasshopper in its web.

# ARACHNIDS
# YELLOW GARDEN SPIDER (ARGIOPE AURANTIA)

Female yellow garden spiders have yellow and black markings on their abdomens. Their legs are brown with black tips. Females can grow to be more than 1 inch (2.5 cm) long. They can be three times larger than males. Males are also less colorful. Their abdomens aren't as vibrant, and their legs are completely brown.

Yellow garden spiders are a type of orb weaver spider. Orb weaver spiders are known for their elaborate webs. Yellow garden spiders make circular webs. There is a zigzag of thick silk that runs through the center of the web. This structure might give the web more stability. The webs are sticky and catch insects. A struggling insect sends vibrations through the web.

A yellow garden spider wraps a moth in spider silk.

Yellow garden spiders are known for their detailed webs.

The spider follows the vibrations to find its prey. Yellow garden spiders remake their webs each night. They eat the sticky silk. Small insects and other matter trapped in the silk provide the spider with nutrients.

## FACT BOX

**Range:** North America, Central America
**Habitat:** Edges of woodlands, plains
**Diet:** Insects

# CENTIPEDES
# AMAZONIAN GIANT CENTIPEDE (SCOLOPENDRA GIGANTEA)

The Amazonian giant centipede has a waxy appearance.

The Amazonian giant centipede is mostly brown. It has a flat back, and its legs have light-yellow bands. It has between 21 and 23 leg pairs. Its rear legs have spines that protect it from predators. Its front legs work like fangs. They inject venom into prey. Like most centipedes, the Amazonian giant centipede has poor vision. Instead, it uses its long antennae to sense prey. The Amazonian giant centipede is the largest centipede species. It grows to be about 12 inches (30 cm) long.

Amazonian giant centipedes must live in humid environments. Otherwise, they will dry out. They are commonly found in the soil and in rotting wood. They are more active at night. These centipedes hunt insects and small animals such as lizards and amphibians. Their venom is strong enough to paralyze and kill prey.

## FACT BOX

**Range**: Northern South America
**Habitat**: Soil, leaf litter, rotting wood
**Diet**: Insects, lizards, amphibians, mice

Amazonian giant centipedes are carnivores.

## CENTIPEDES
# BARK CENTIPEDE (SCOLOPOCRYPTOPS SEXSPINOSUS)

A bark centipede protects her young.

Bark centipedes have yellow legs and reddish-brown, flat bodies. Their flat bodies help them squeeze into tight spaces. Their feet have barbs that help them grip their prey. Adults can grow to up to 2 inches (5 cm) long.

Bark centipedes primarily eat insects and other small animals. They are more active at night. They are often found near trees in search of prey. They can also be found in moist,

dark spaces such as cellars. Because of their small size, most bark centipedes are not strong enough to bite humans. If they do bite a person, the reaction is usually not severe. It is comparable to a bee sting. It may cause some pain and swelling.

### FACT BOX
**Range:** Eastern North America
**Habitat:** Near trees, moist and dark places
**Diet:** Insects, other small animals

Bark centipedes explore logs and trees in search of food.

# CENTIPEDES
# GIANT DESERT CENTIPEDE (SCOLOPENDRA HEROS)

The giant desert centipede has a black body and yellow legs. It has a red head and antennae. The bright colors signal that the centipede is venomous. It has between 21 and 23 leg pairs. It can grow to be as long as 8 inches (20 cm). It is the largest centipede species in North America.

Despite its name, the giant desert centipede does not live only in deserts. It can be found in a variety of environments in the southern United States and Mexico. In addition to deserts, it can be found in warm, moist environments and seashores. Giant desert centipedes live under stones

Giant desert centipedes have yellow legs that warn predators that they are venomous.

and logs. A female lays her eggs in rotting wood. She protects her young until they are able to care for themselves.

Giant desert centipedes can be aggressive. They may bite and pinch humans. Their legs can cut human skin. They may secrete venom into these wounds. Their venom can cause pain and swelling but is not typically fatal.

**FACT BOX**

**Range:** Mexico, southern United States
**Habitat:** Deserts, seashores, warm and moist areas
**Diet:** Insects, lizards, mice

Giant desert centipedes are also called giant red-headed centipedes.

# CENTIPEDES
# HOUSE CENTIPEDE (SCUTIGERA COLEOPTRATA)

The house centipede has three dark stripes that run along the length of its brown body. It has 15 leg pairs. Its legs and antennae are long and thin. The last pair of legs on an adult female centipede can be twice the length of its body. The house centipede does not have a flattened body like

House centipedes sense prey with their long antennae.

other centipedes. This allows it to move quickly. These centipedes are relatively small. Excluding its legs and antennae, it grows only to be around 1 inch (2.5 cm) long.

House centipedes prefer dark, damp places. They can be found under rocks and logs. But they are also commonly spotted in homes. They may enter basements and bathrooms during the winter to escape the cold. Many people are frightened by these centipedes, but they are important creatures. They eat insects and control the number of household pests such as cockroaches, silverfish, and bed bugs.

House centipedes sometimes crawl through unused drains.

**FACT BOX**
**Range:** Mediterranean, United States, Mexico
**Habitat:** Dark, moist places
**Diet:** Insects, spiders

## MILLIPEDES
# AMERICAN GIANT MILLIPEDE (NARCEUS AMERICANUS)

Millipedes curl up into balls when they are threatened.

The American giant millipede has a thick, black body with reddish-orange edges. It grows to around 4 inches (10 cm) long. The American giant millipede has sensitive antennae. It uses its antennae to taste and smell. It is the most common millipede species in North America. A female of this species lays one egg at a time. She protects the egg until it hatches.

All millipede species eat decaying matter. They help nutrients return to the soil. They do not tend to gather in groups and are not aggressive.

Millipede species have many ways to protect themselves against predators. They are able to coil into a ball. This protects their legs and heads. Only their tough exoskeletons are exposed. The American giant millipede can also release a smelly chemical. This warns predators to stay away.

**FACT BOX**

**Range:** Eastern United States
**Habitat:** Forests, farmlands
**Diet:** Decaying plants, wood

American giant millipedes can live up to 11 years.

# MILLIPEDES
# GIANT AFRICAN MILLIPEDE (ARCHISPIROSTREPTUS GIGAS)

The giant African millipede has a dark-brown or black body. It is the largest millipede species in the world. It can grow to around 12 inches (30 cm) long. A full-grown giant African millipede may have more than 40 body segments and as many as 400 legs. Each body segment has a hole called a spiracle. Millipedes use spiracles to breathe. If spiracles fill with water, millipedes will drown.

Young giant African millipedes do not have as many body segments. They are white when they first hatch. They have only three pairs of legs at this time. They add legs and body segments as they molt. They molt for the first time within the first 12 hours of hatching.

Giant African millipedes eat decaying plants. They help nutrients return to the soil. This fertilizes the soil and keeps the soil healthy.

The giant African millipede can taste with all parts of its body.

## FACT BOX
**Range:** Western Africa
**Habitat:** Rain forests
**Diet:** Decaying organic matter

The giant African millipede moves slowly.

# MILLIPEDES
# GREENHOUSE MILLIPEDE (OXIDUS GRACILIS)

Greenhouse millipedes have black or brown bodies and white legs. They have about 15 body segments and around 60 legs when fully grown. They can grow to be 1 inch (2.5 cm) long. They continue to grow and add body segments until they reach adulthood.

Hundreds of greenhouse millipedes may cluster together to breed.

Greenhouse millipedes are native to Asia. They are invasive to Europe and the Americas. The species earned its name for its ability to thrive in greenhouses. These millipedes prefer warm, moist environments. They also do not have any predators in greenhouses. There is also plenty of plant material to eat. Greenhouse millipedes eat only decaying plant matter, so they do not harm plants.

The greenhouse millipede can produce a smelly odor. It signals to predators that these millipedes are poisonous. They are harmless to humans. But the scent can be overwhelming when there is a large number of greenhouse millipedes.

A greenhouse millipede curls up to protect itself.

## FACT BOX

**Range:** Asia, Europe, North America, South America
**Habitat:** Hot, humid places, such as greenhouses or in decaying logs
**Diet:** Decaying organic matter

## MILLIPEDES
# WHITE-LEGGED SNAKE MILLIPEDE (TACHYPODOIULUS NIGER)

**W**hite-legged snake millipedes have jet-black bodies. Their legs are bright white. They have about 100 legs and up to 56 body segments. They are approximately 2.7 inches (7 cm) long when full grown.

These millipedes are common throughout Europe. They may be found in woodlands and near compost piles. Like other millipede species, the white-legged snake millipede feeds on decaying plant matter. It helps recycle nutrients to the soil. It may also eat fruits such as raspberries and strawberries.

White-legged snake millipedes eat only plant material.

White-legged snake millipedes can be seen crawling through gardens.

White-legged snake millipedes are most active at night. During the day, they may hide under rocks or burrow under the soil. Being nocturnal may help millipedes avoid predators such as birds and hedgehogs. They can also curl up to protect their heads and legs. Like many millipede species, white-legged snake millipedes produce a smelly chemical to warn predators to stay away.

### FACT BOX

**Range:** Europe
**Habitat:** Woodlands, leaf litter, under rocks and logs
**Diet:** Decaying organic matter

# GLOSSARY

**burrow**
An underground tunnel.

**camouflage**
The ability to blend into one's surroundings because of coloring or pattern.

**colony**
A large population of the same insect species that shares a nest.

**infest**
To spread or gather in large numbers, causing damage or other problems.

**larva**
The earliest life stage for some insects, often worm-like in appearance.

**mandibles**
The mouthparts or jaws used to bite or eat food.

**molt**
To shed an exoskeleton for a larger one.

**nymph**
The young stage of certain insects that has a different appearance than its adult form.

**pest**
An animal or plant that causes significant problems for humans.

**pollinator**
An animal that carries pollen between flowering plants.

**predator**
An animal that attacks and kills another animal for food.

**prey**
An animal that is eaten by another animal.

**scavenger**
An animal that primarily eats dead animals.

**swarm**
A large group of insects, especially those that fly.

**venom**
A toxic chemical used to injure or kill prey.

# TO LEARN MORE

## FURTHER READINGS

Evans, Christine. *The Evolution of Insects*. Abdo, 2019.

Honovich, Nancy. *1,000 Facts about Insects*. National Geographic, 2018.

Mooney, Carla. *Insects and Arachnids*. Abdo, 2022.

## ONLINE RESOURCES

To learn more about bugs, please visit **abdobooklinks.com** or scan this QR code. These links are routinely monitored and updated to provide the most current information available.

# INDEX

abdomens, 5–6, 8, 10, 20, 38, 64, 116, 134, 142, 146, 154, 162–163, 166, 168, 170
Africa, 47, 50–51, 87, 133, 147, 149, 182
ambush predators, 98, 106, 158, 160
ants, 6, 24–25, 34–35, 127
aphids, 13, 25, 42, 78–79, 98, 123
arachnids, 5, 7, 134–171
Asia, 17, 32, 43, 45, 47, 52, 53, 54, 55, 61, 87, 107, 135, 185
Australia, 18–19, 43, 65, 101, 151, 163

bees, 50–51, 82–83, 93
beetles, 6, 28–29, 52–53, 68–69, 70, 74–75, 76–77, 80–81, 90–91, 112–113, 116–117, 122–123
burrows, 4, 56, 64–65, 77, 102, 111, 112, 117, 139, 149, 153, 157, 160–161, 187
butterflies, 6, 44–45, 54–55, 72–73, 86, 100–101

camouflage, 44, 66–67, 75, 104–105, 107, 135
caterpillars, 16, 42, 54–55, 73, 88–89, 97, 101, 114–115, 118–119, 120–121, 126–127
centipedes, 5–7, 172–179
Central America, 29, 51, 69, 73, 81, 129, 131, 133, 171
cockroaches, 8–9, 64–65
colonies, 20, 24, 34, 43, 51, 60–61, 70, 82–83
crickets, 56–57, 102–103

deserts, 47, 129, 142, 143, 147, 161, 169, 176, 177
diseases, 7, 22, 48, 63, 79, 85, 133, 137

eggs, 11, 20, 23, 26–27, 28, 38–39, 41, 49, 53, 62, 65, 67, 69, 70, 75, 84, 93, 101, 102, 111, 112, 117, 120, 128–129, 131, 132, 139, 151, 161, 177, 180
endangered species, 56, 95, 165
Europe, 41, 43, 56, 59, 87, 116, 117, 155, 167, 185, 186, 187

flies, 12–13, 36, 40–41, 62–63, 84–85

grasshoppers, 10–11, 38–39, 48, 108–109
grubs, 76–77, 91, 123

habitat loss, 56, 101

infestations, 23, 28, 33, 48, 53, 62, 78–79, 91, 125, 167
invasive species, 32, 52, 90, 91, 95, 185

larvae, 13, 15, 20, 27, 28, 36, 38, 53, 69, 70, 75, 76–77, 82, 91, 93, 112, 117, 129, 133, 136
live young, 65, 149

mating processes, 17, 40–41, 58, 69, 70, 74, 80–81, 88, 106–107, 111, 114, 118, 139, 162–163
Mexico, 11, 27, 29, 100, 131, 153, 161, 176, 177, 179

millipedes, 5–7, 180–187
moths, 16–17, 86–87, 88–89, 96–97, 114–115, 118–119, 120–121, 126–127

nests, 20, 24, 26–27, 43, 51, 60, 93
North America, 13, 20, 25, 51, 71, 75, 81, 89, 99, 101, 102, 105, 109, 119, 133, 137, 155, 171, 175, 176, 180, 185

pests, 7, 22, 28, 42–43, 49, 55, 62, 79, 99, 117, 123, 125, 141, 144, 151, 166, 179
pollinators, 7, 13, 42, 50, 83, 155

scavengers, 36, 41
scorpions, 5, 146–147, 148–149, 158–159
South America, 31, 51, 69, 73, 81, 99, 101, 129, 131, 133, 157, 173, 185
spiders, 5, 127, 134–135, 138–139, 140–141, 144–145, 150–151, 154–155, 156–157, 160–161, 162–163, 168–169, 170–171

tarantulas, 128–129, 138–139, 156–157, 160–161, 164–165

venom, 6, 20, 26, 35, 89, 121, 126, 128, 141, 147, 148, 151, 152, 156, 158–159, 161, 164–165, 168–169, 172–173, 176–177

wasps, 26–27, 42–43, 92–93, 128–129

# PHOTO CREDITS

Cover Photos: Bonnie Taylor Barry/Shutterstock, front (atlas moth); Shutterstock, front (walking stick), front (wasp), front (fly), front (locust), front (millipede); Melinda Fawver/Shutterstock, front (ant), back (ant); Eric Isselee/Shutterstock, front (scorpion), back (Hercules beetle); Deep Desert Photography/Shutterstock, front (centipede); James Laurie/Shutterstock, back (luna moth); Ernie Cooper/Shutterstock, front (black widow)
Interior Photos: Bo Valentino/Shutterstock, 3, 5, 161; Eric Isselee/Shutterstock, 4 (top), 56, 67, 148; Jay Ondreicka/Shutterstock, 4 (bottom), 168; Matt Jeppson/Shutterstock, 6, 114; Conrad Barrington/Shutterstock, 7 (top); Daniel Prudek/Shutterstock, 7 (bottom); Shutterstock, 8, 10, 20, 23, 32, 36, 40, 44, 45, 49, 51, 52, 54, 55, 59, 61, 64, 66, 68, 70–71, 71, 72, 73, 75, 77, 79, 80, 82, 84, 86, 87, 97, 101, 104–105, 106, 116, 117, 123, 124–125, 130, 132, 133, 134, 137, 138, 139, 150, 151, 155, 156, 164, 169, 172, 183; Vinicius R. Souza/Shutterstock, 9, 85; Melinda Fawver/Shutterstock, 11; Paul Reeves Photography/Shutterstock, 12, 27; Judy Gallagher/Flickr, 13, 113; Taste Of Crayons/Wikimedia, 14; Mike Lucibella/NSF/USAP, 15; Vladimir Sazonov/Shutterstock, 16–17; Ron Eldie/Shutterstock, 17; Aedka Studio/Shutterstock, 18–19; Claudia Evans/Shutterstock, 19; Karel Bock/Shutterstock, 21; Akos Nagy/Shutterstock, 22; Meister Photos/Shutterstock, 24, 171; Elliotte Rusty Harold/Shutterstock, 25; Pascal Guay/Shutterstock, 26; George D. Lepp/Science Source, 28; Agriculture Research Service/USDA/Wikimedia, 29; Patrick Landmann/Science Source, 30–31; Dante Fenolio/Science Source, 31; Davide Bonora/Shutterstock, 33; Francesco Tomasinelli/Science Source, 34; Andres Nunez Mora/Shutterstock, 35; Robert Adami/Shutterstock, 37, 41; James Urbach/SuperStock, 38; Brett Hondow/Shutterstock, 38–39, 98, 126; Pavel Rumlena/Shutterstock, 42; Jonas Vegele/Shutterstock, 43; Jen Watson/Shutterstock, 46; Holger Kirk/Shutterstock, 47; Nigel Cattlin/Science Source, 48, 166, 185; Lian van den Heever/Shutterstock, 50; Elena Berd/Shutterstock, 53; Hans Reinhard/Science Source, 57; Lauren Suryanata/Shutterstock, 58; Dan Olsen/Shutterstock, 60, 165; Anne Webber/Shutterstock, 62; Hermann Eisenbeiss/Science Source, 63; Goddard Photography/iStockphoto, 65; Phil Degginger/Science Source, 69; Simon Shim/Shutterstock, 74, 135, 178; Scott Camazine/Science Source, 76, 141, 170; Scott Bauer/Agriculture Research Service/USDA/Wikimedia, 78; Pete Oxford/Minden Pictures/SuperStock, 81; Terrie L. Zeller/Shutterstock, 83; Michael P. Gadomski/Science Source, 88; Bella Vita Images/Shutterstock, 89; Mircea Costina/Shutterstock, 90; NSC Photography/Shutterstock, 91; Yunhyok Choi/Shutterstock, 92; Jean and Fred Hort/Flickr, 93; iStockphoto, 94; Louise Murray/Science Source, 95; Candia Baxter/Shutterstock, 96; Chase D'animulls/Shutterstock, 99; Maria T. Hoffman/Shutterstock, 100; Andy Reago & Chrissy McClarren/Flickr, 102, 120; Animals Animals/SuperStock, 103; Stefano Buttafoco/Shutterstock, 104; Vince Adam/Shutterstock, 107; Rose Ludwig/Shutterstock, 108; Gerry Bishop/Shutterstock, 109; Jeff Herge/Shutterstock, 110; Susan Law Cain/Shutterstock, 111; James H. Robinson/Science Source, 112; Michael Pettigrew/Shutterstock, 114–115; Rachel E. Sullivan/Shutterstock, 118; Gary Meszaros/Science Source, 119; Steve Byland/Shutterstock, 121; Protasov An/Shutterstock, 122, 146, 147; Eleon Images/Shutterstock, 124; Liz Weber/Shutterstock, 127; D. A. Boyd/Shutterstock, 128; Charles Sharp/Flickr, 129; Stephen Dalton/Minden Pictures/SuperStock, 131; Erik Karits/Shutterstock, 136–137; Sari O'Neal/Shutterstock, 140; Sinclair Stammers/Science Source, 142; Viktor Loki/Shutterstock, 143; Csabo Photo/Shutterstock, 144–145; Olivier Laurent Photos/Shutterstock, 145; ZSSD/Minden Pictures/SuperStock, 149; Guillermo Guerao Serra/Shutterstock, 152, 153; Henrik Larsson/Shutterstock, 154; Audrey Snider-Bell/Shutterstock, 156–157; Reality Images/Shutterstock, 158, 158–159; Ernie Cooper/Shutterstock, 160; Adam Fletcher/Biosphoto/SuperStock, 162; Adam Fletcher/Biosphoto/Science Source, 163; Jonathan Oscar/Shutterstock, 167; Tom McHugh/Science Source, 173; Nature's Images/Science Source, 174–175; John Serrao/Science Source, 175; Scott Delony/Shutterstock, 176; Cathleen Wake Gorbatenko/Shutterstock, 177; Jon Osumi/Shutterstock, 179; Kate Short/Shutterstock, 180; Jeff Caughey/Shutterstock, 181; Piotr Naskrecki/Minden Pictures/SuperStock, 182–183; Ivan Kuzmin/Science Source, 184; Sandra Standbridge/Shutterstock, 186–187; Frank Ramspott/iStockphoto, 187

**ABDOBOOKS.COM**

Published by Abdo Publishing, a division of ABDO, PO Box 398166, Minneapolis, Minnesota 55439. Copyright © 2023 by Abdo Consulting Group, Inc. International copyrights reserved in all countries. No part of this book may be reproduced in any form without written permission from the publisher. Abdo Reference™ is a trademark and logo of Abdo Publishing.

Printed in the United States of America, North Mankato, Minnesota.
052022
092022

Editor: Angela Lim
Series Designer: Colleen McLaren
Content Consultant: Brian Aukema, PhD; Professor, University of Minnesota

**LIBRARY OF CONGRESS CONTROL NUMBER: 2021952343**

**PUBLISHER'S CATALOGING-IN-PUBLICATION DATA**
Names: Marquardt, Meg, author.
Title: The bug encyclopedia / by Meg Marquardt
Description: Minneapolis, Minnesota: Abdo Publishing, 2023 | Series: Science encyclopedias | Includes online resources and index.
Identifiers: ISBN 9781532198748 (lib. bdg.) | ISBN 9781098272395 (ebook)
Subjects: LCSH: Insects--Juvenile literature. | Entomology--Juvenile literature. | Zoology—Juvenile literature. | Encyclopedias and dictionaries--Juvenile literature.
Classification: DDC 595.7--dc23